The
COMPLEAT
Eel~Gutting
~ Guide Booke ~

Dad, I'd 86 this stupid eel concept. The book hasn't even started yet!

DON'T LISTEN TO HER, ABADEER! EELS ARE RAD! Speshly if they're Electric.

An Official Publication of the Land of Ooo Swamp-fishing
and Sports-memorabilia Cabal, and Not at All a Decoy Title Page
to Throw Off Enemies Who May Want to Steal this Precious Book,
or to Trick Unqualified Readers by Boring
Them with What Appears to Be an Incredibly Dull,
Dreary, and Tedious Outdoorsy Book That No
Sentient Creature, No Matter How Dim-witted,
Would Ever Ever *Ever* Want to Read, Never Mind Even Think
About Turning to the Next Page for Fear of Falling Asleep due to
what appears to be an Utterly Uninteresting and Incredibly Lame Series of
Texts Composed of Bland, Unexciting, Pedestrian, Mind-numbing,
and Bogus Descriptions Told in Excruciatingly
Sleep-inducing Detail.

WARNING

Only Bona Fide Demons from the Nightosphere, Heroes with Extreme Charisma, Wizards with Abominable Powers, and Awesome Kingly or Queenly Individuals may read further. All Unqualified Readers—including Humans, Mutants, Monsters, Talking Beasts, House People, Gnomes and Goblins, Mountain Men, Lumps, Witches, Ninjas, Hoboes, Ghosts, Scofflaws, Insolent Children, Boring Schoolteachers, Nosy Parents, and other Unqualified Beings—will be punished by the Spell of Carnak invoked upon this Book. As a result of the Spell, YOU, Unqualified Reader, will become more and more confused as you read. By Book II, you will go into a dull stupor, and by Book III, you will start twitching uncontrollably. And if you persevere in your Insolence and read Book IV, you will violently mutate into a Giant Mucous Worm, quickly become encased in an insect-like Cocoon of Aetheric Phlegm, and die, doomed to float invisibly through the Aether as a Ghost in the Land of Ooo, attracted only by the Stench of Roadkill, until Time is a Flickering Shadow and the World of Talking Beings has been muffled by the Blanket of Oblivion.

BEWARE, UNQUALIFIED READERS!
STOP READING NOW!
YOU HAVE BEEN WARNED!

Um, Dad, might wanna dial down the grosstitude. And all these ten-dollar words are getting annoying.

GROSS IS FREAKIN' COOL!

Sicker the Better, baby!

THE AUTHOR AND HIS DAUGHTER

THE REAL TITLE PAGE

of the

PRICELESS, BRILLIANT, *and* INEFFABLE ™

ENCYCLOPÆDIA OF THE LAND OF OOO

INCLUDING ITS

INHABITANTS, LORE, SPELLS, *and* ANCIENT CRYPT WARNINGS

CIRCA *19.56 B.G.E. – 501 A.G.E.*

COMPILED, WRITTEN, and PAINSTAKINGLY EDITED by

HUNSON ABADEER

AKA *LORD of EVIL,*

AKA *THE NAMELESS ONE,*

WHOSE UNNAMEABLENESS MAKES THE JUNK MAIL of ETERNITY UNDELIVERABLE

TRANSLATED from the SCROLLS of OOO by

MARTIN OLSON

NOTED LINGUIST of NIGHTOSPHEREAN TONGUES

ART AND ENGRAVING RESTORATIONS
BY THE FORMIDABLE DEMONIC ARTISTS
RENEE FRENCH, TONY MILLIONAIRE, CELESTE MORENO,
AISLEEN ROMANO, AND MAHENDRA SINGH
PUBLISHED IN THIS COMMEMORATIVE FACSIMILE EDITION
BY TITAN BOOKS, LONDON

TABLE OF CONTENTS

BOOK III
THE LAND OF OOO AND YOU
TO BE READ in the DEEPEST TONES of SARCASM

BOOK IV
THE LOST TEXTS OF OOO
IN WHICH the UNSPEAKABLE is SPOKEN

BOOK V
FORBIDDEN CHAPTERS
IN THE ENCYCLOPÆDIA OF OOO

GOING BACKWARD
FOREWORD

This Foreword is written in a backward manner, designed to test the Fortitude and Worthiness of, as well as to Annoy, the Reader, and by way of providing a Formal initiation through which the Reader must Engage the backward reading of this Precious Text. Only the most Diligent, Courageous, and Stalwart Alphabet Absorbers will even bother to continue reading in such an initiating, time-consuming manner as reading backward, and even you want to stop but somehow find that you must go on for missing the Secret Material that surely must be included at the end rather, in this case, at the Beginning of this Backward Foreword. However, in fact, there is no Secret to Be Revealed at the end at All. This is Only a Practical Device to Journey you the Reader, to make you Worthy of Further Reading. For it is Only by overcoming the Aggravation of this decidedly sharing and off-putting literary drudgery that one can qualify to be a Reader of Hidden Secrets. And since you are not about to reach the, or rather, the Beginning, you have now Proven Yourself Worthy of this Encyclopaedia of the Land of Ooo and its Priceless Secrets Hidden Herein. The End.

LORD OF EVIL IN REPOSE

PREFACE REGARDING NO ONE

As the Author and Compiler of the *Encyclopaedia of Ooo*, forthwith I briefly and incisively introduce Myself to You, my Demon Readers whose Souls have not yet been sucked out. I am most comfortably addressed as Hunson Abadeer, or Marceline's dad, although I have also been called Lord of Evil, The Nameless One, The Faceless Enigma, or, in my youth as a carny boss, Johnny Corndog.

What's up with these mysterious names? The answer is simple. I am incredibly mysterious. I do not, after all, know my own Origin, who I am, or how I emerged from Nothingness into the Annoying Land of Ooo. I only know that before arriving here I existed Forever, before the Vast and Ineluctable Scope of My Memory began. Believe me, a bad memory is a major hassle if you're a Supremely Evil Being. Not knowing who I am or why I am here tends to make me a tad grouchy. Totes on that!

My single earliest memory occurred eons before the Mushroom War. This memory consists of one image: me eating a ham sandwich, perched atop Rock Candy Mountain, overlooking the Sea of Something, long before Plants, Animals, and Actual Things came into existence in the Land of Ooo, surrounded by an all-encompassing Night of Nothingness.

WOW...HER DAD KNOWS SQUAT Dude, he's JBH.

Full disclosure: I believe I was a ghost at the time, although it isn't clear how a ghost can sit on a mountain peak or eat a ham sandwich. But who cares? I'm here, I'm pumped, and I'm ready to suck souls. What else really matters? *Pops, I'd cut the sandwich refs. NOBODY CARES what you eat.*

One more thing. In reading this Encyclopaedia, you will perceive the two primal aspects of my personality: *I only CARE if he eats ME!*

the part that taps into the Radiant Brilliance of Evil, using big words and despising all beings equally...

...and the part of me that taps into the Earthy Plebian Mind of a typical, lowbrow, worthless, know-nothing Oooian.

OOOOH I'M SHAKIN' ABADEER!

Make no mistake, both parts of me will still suck the soul-essence from You the Reader—when I have the chance. So watch your back.

And with this string of words I conclude this Preface About Myself.

Hey Pops! Rad pictures!!

Ad Finem.

HEY, THERE'S NONE OF ME!

HERE'S ONE

Quit it, you're wrecking the resale value!

COMPOSING THE ENCYCLOPÆDIA OF OOO

INTRODUCTION
TO THE
INTRODUCTION

The only existing pages of the Introduction to the *Encyclopaedia of the Land of Ooo* were ripped out of the original copy of This Book by the Ancient King Aaa of Ooo and accidentally burned to ashes in the Conflagrations of the Great Mushroom War. Hidden in the text of this Original Introduction, via the conceit of microscopic letters visible only to Wizards, was the text of the *entire book.*

The rest of the Original Encyclopaedia was padded with random words having the overall semblance of sense but clothed in mind-numbing dullness to throw off enemy spies and to confuse ignorant Giants, unpleasant schoolteachers, and nosy, know-it-all parents. Why was the book hidden in a seemingly insane manner? As a security measure, of course. This book is too important to be read by idiots. Since no one ever reads introductions (including this one), the entire encyclopaedia was safely hidden.

A single word "the," the only surviving scrap of the original introduction, is stored in a vault in the Museum of Ooo Artifacts and Sugary Confections. It is the only existing artifact from ancient times before the Mushroom War. Scholars, Experts, and other Ignorant Quacksalvers disagree over the word's symbolism and have, through the centuries, assassinated each another, attempting to have the Last Word. Though I commend these murderous scholars, nothing more will be said in this book regarding this ancient alphabetical remnant, so I hope you were paying attention.[1]

Thus concludes this Introductory Introduction and the reason for its existence. Know, O Reader, that this Introduction shall never, ever be referred to again in the Future History of Ooo, except in the words concluding this sentence, and know that its last mention, before it winks out of existence, is in the self-same words you are reading right now.

Think so, Dude.

Did he just call us idiots?

No offense, Dad, but BO-O-ORING

YEAH, BUT IT'S WEIRD ENOUGH SO YOU DON'T FALL ASLEEP. *Sez you. ZzZzZz*

I

WORTHLESS INHABITANTS OF THE LAND OF OOO

WHOSE SOULS I SHALL REFRAIN *from* SUCKING OUT *in* DEFERENCE *to my* DAUGHTER

As Lord of Evil, it is part of my job description to despise all paltry inhabitants of the Land of Ooo, who are at best Insignificant Gnats and at worst Annoying Flesh-tubes Oozing with Gore.

However, I begin with the Personages of Ooo who are, IMHO, the least annoying, and then go on to enumerate the detestable rank-and-file Oooians whose souls I pledge to suck dry like a hungry confectioner sucking sugar-icing from a cake squeezer.

Here, then, are the Main Personalities weaving through the Tapestry of Tim,[2] and also the Tapestry of Time, in the Land of Ooo, Past, Present, and Future.

FINN THE HUMAN

FINN THE HUMAN

This obnoxious, spindly-armed human boy, O Reader, is the last human in existence after the Great Mushroom War. Despite his throw-up–inducing essence, *Finn the Human is the second most important personage in all of Ooo.* For when I squint my eyes and scan the Wobbly Wheel of Future Time, it appears that Finn the Human bears a Powerful Secret in his heart (or under his armpits—I forget which) that will transform the destiny of all inhabitants of the Land of Ooo. Then again, I may have gotten that all wrong. He might simply screw up, get distracted, start his obnoxious beat-boxing, and forget The Secret entirely. But if he *doesn't*, well, look, just keep an eye on him, all right? My natural tendency is to despise him and instantly suck out his soul, but I'll forgo that for the time being because my daughter likes him.

ADDITIONAL DATA

Teeth: A few missing, due to his imbecilic propensity to chew on rocks, tree trunks, and dead lizards.

Eyes: From a distance, dungeon black. Close-up, frozen-cow-udder blue. When he's hypnotized, his left eye turns green, so don't hypnotize him if crazy eyes freak you out.

Hair: Absurdly blond and absurdly long. When he removes his hat with a flourish, his gender becomes an impenetrable mystery. Note: As Supreme Arbiter of Evil in the Nightosphere, I realize it is unseemly that I write about this nincompoop's hair. Know, O Reader, that it was not my idea. Blame my daughter!

FINN THE HUMAN'S HISTORY

Finn the Human is a foundling, which means he was *found* someplace. In this case, he was found as an infant in the mysterious East Oooian Woodlands by a family of filthy runt-dogs. His biological parents, who will never be mentioned again in this book, inexplicably ran away. Typical cowardly human swine. Who'd abandon something as cute and adorable as a human baby in the woods, instead of selling or eating it?[3]

The story I heard was this: While traversing the woodland, a filthy dog couple found Baby Finn crawling through the dirt like an oversize slug. A diapered slug filled with boom-boom. The dog couple had never seen a human before and thought he was a bizarre species of mudfish. And that, O Demon Reader, is why they called him Finn!

So the runt-dog couple took him home, probably thinking they'd boil and eat him. But when they found he didn't have fins at all and instead

had funny, floppy arms and legs that twisted around like pretzels, the dogs did what any normal creatures would—they laughed at him! And because he was worth a few laughs, they decided not to boil and eat him. Instead, as strange as it sounds to me, they decided to adopt him and love him. And thus their hybrid family was born, and their dog sons Jake and Jermaine became Finn's brothers.

How to Recognize Finn the Human

Aside from the tedious pictures of this *Fool of Flesh* within these *Pages*, here's a graph of Finn's basic I.D. Breakdown:

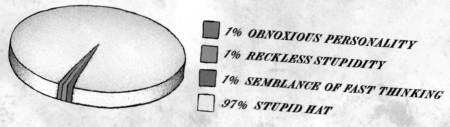

- 1% **OBNOXIOUS PERSONALITY**
- 1% **RECKLESS STUPIDITY**
- 1% **SEMBLANCE OF FAST THINKING**
- 97% **STUPID HAT**

When they brought Finn home to their filthy hovel, he *was* pretty entertaining. For example, in the months that followed, as Baby Finn began to speak, the toddler would stand up on his tiny feet and sing ridiculous songs he made up in a high, baby voice while waggling his tiny behind:

I'm a buff baby
That can dance like a man!
I can shake-ah my booty,
I can shake-ah my can!

I'm a tough, tootin' baby!
I can punch-a yo' buns,
Punch-a yo' buns,
I can punch all yo' buns!
If you're an evil witch,
I will punch you for fun!

Baby Finn's absurd, waggling butt-dance accompanying this song is articulated in the following diagram:

And believe it or not, this human and his family of canine fools became as close as a family of filthy Oooians can be. Especially Finn and his
dog-bro Jake. They got along so well, it almost seemed they were destined
to be in the same litter. When Finn grew up to be a teenager, Jake became
his best friend. Henceforth, O Reader, know that those two dudes are
tight, man. FOR REALS!

In fact, nothing in, above or below the Land of Ooo could *ever* come
between that dog and that human. *Nothing.*[4]

FINN THE HUMAN'S PERSONALITY

Know, O Demon Reader, that this tube of flesh is a typically moronic human. He ignores mortal danger if there is the slightest whiff of fun to be had. His stupidity is matched only by his arrogance in thinking he is a Gift to the Ladies, the most obnoxious human trait in existence. The depiction at left shows Finn at a party where the narcissistic fool was given the moniker "Prince Hotbod."

More than anything, Finn's repulsive personality seems to be attracted to *adventure*. His folly is such that he enjoys almost being killed, because, as rumor has it, he thinks escaping at the last instant is *fun*. I would urge, you, Demon Reader, not to follow suit, unless you wish to Merge with the Void. This begs the question: Why does Finn the Human not die after putting himself in the path of ridiculous danger over and over again? Answer: Something about Finn the Human is, shall we say, *indestructible*, as detestable a concept as an *immortal human* is to me personally. In fact, let's change the subject and speak no more of him, shall we?

Oh, wait a minute. My daughter Marceline asked me as a favor to include a few more details about this inept and spindly human boy. To accommodate her, I include the following deleterious material:

Thanks, Dad. Finn's cool!

WE'RE BFF, MARCELINE!

PHOBIAS

what about ME?

Thalassophobia. Which means, O Ignorant Reader, "fear of the ocean." Waves and sea foam? Forget about it! The mindless boy *hates* them. The tiniest spatter of the sea spray erases all rational thought. It's a conundrum, for my spies tell me that he is not afraid of taking a bath or drinking a glass of H_2O. So what's up with his knees knocking in terror when a piddling drop of salt water hits his gooning face?

Good question. And the answer is: *Who cares?* He's a meaningless human being, a dolt, a future pile of dust, tantamount to Nothing. You shall either find out someday why he hates water *or you won't*. Simply get it through your head, O Curious Reader, that this lowly flesh-pod is anti-aquatic to the max.

SICKENING, UNSPEAKABLE CRUSHES

Like all human boys, Finn has had numerous idiotic crushes, including an endless, unrequited adoration of the unbearably cute Princess Bubblegum and a rebound fixation on the temperamental Flame Princess. However, shall we move on? This topic sickens me.

One thing I may say in the ignorant fool's favor, he has the same natural reaction all boys have when confronted with *romance*: If he sees a kissing scene in a movie, he clutches his stomach and starts to dry-heave. Then he not only vomits his breakfast, lunch, and dinner, but in addition *yesterday's* breakfast, lunch, and dinner. Thus human boys have one and only one good quality—retching at the abomination of love.

WHAT FINN THE HUMAN WANTS

Easy. He wants to be the greatest Hero in the History of Ooo. Too bad he's handicapped by being a human whose intelligence score peaks at Imbecile Level.

HEY, I'M NO IMBESILE!

Nice, Finn. Spell much?

Miscellaneous Characteristics: Although he generally exhibits mindless stupidity, it is rumored that Finn the Human, at times, appears to have an exceedingly powerful imagination.

Like all humans since the beginning of time, but before they were extinct, Finn is exceedingly stubborn, can be easily tricked, loses his temper, behaves like a moron, feels guilty a lot, likes to work hard and play hard, makes stupid origami animals, and is gifted at hocking phlegm.[5]

I'm starting to like this Book. Lots of spitting and barfing.

I CAN'T WAIT TO SEE WHAT HE SAYS ABOUT YOU.

[TEN RUMORS CONCERNING FINN THE HUMAN]

Eat a Bowl of my drool! hahaha

1. His favorite food is meat loaf. Ugh.
2. Finn has *heterochromia*. Look it up, O Lazy, Demonic Dunce!
3. My daughter informed me that Finn actually *likes* an inane pink sweater Princess Bubblegum gave him, and keeps a lock of her tawdry hair. *HA HA HA!* A colorful happenstance, however pathetic. *AWK-WARD, DUDE!* *SHUT UP!!*
4. While this admission is beneath me, I heard through the grapevine that when his trousers were stolen, it was evident Finn wears tighty whiteys.
5. Unlike other humans, Finn has the uncanny ability to make fire with his bare hands, and thus is capable of roasting wienies without a campfire. (I am aware this is boring, but I still have five more tawdry facts to go.)

6. According to my daughter's reports, Finn can apparently bend his arms in ridiculous if not repulsive ways, waving them in the air like strands of flopping spaghetti.

7. When he signed the Nightosphere Guest Book, I noted Finn has the Befuddled Curse of Left-Handedness, denoting a brain wired with inept circuitry. (I am right-handed; thus all Left-Handers are inferior.)

8. A reliable informant who asked not to be identified stated that, after accidentally swallowing a minuscule computer, Finn developed the ghastly ability to auto-tune his voice at will.

9. The same informer further revealed that Finn believes that his beat-boxing abilities are the greatest in the Land of Ooo. Since he has never heard me beat-box, he has never heard the greatest of all. *EAT A DIRTY SOCK, ABADEER!*

10. Finn the Human has committed the *I CHALLENGE YOU!* abomination of spitting on my daughter, and for that he will someday suffer the *YEAH!!!* Unspeakable Wrath of Hunson Abadeer, Lord of Evil.

WHAT A JERK. I WAS JUST KIDDING AROUND.

I have spoken. *I know, right?*

He's got some ego issues.

JAKE THE DOG

JAKE THE DOG

Who cares about a filthy, stinking, mongrel mutt? Answer: *I do*. Simply because I'm Lord of Evil doesn't mean I don't like cute doggies. Unfortunately, Finn the Human loves the mutt in question, who is in fact his adopted brother Jake.

Why the love? Who knows why. After all, Jake the Dog is a directionless, lazy, canine, couch-potato slacker. Too lazy to even chase, eat, and digest cats. In his monumental laziness, he even refuses to rise from the sofa to go to the bathroom and instead he will simply lift his leg without getting up and, to speak indelicately, he will then ga~~~~~~~~~

~~~~~~~~~~~~~~~~~~~~~~~~~~~~

HARSH!!!

TOLD YA!

Dude, this is stupid. I'm crossing it out!

IT WAS STUPID. AND TRUE!

Although the subject of this dog bores me to tears, let me get past the basics so I may gratefully move on: Via Demonic Fact-checking, we have gleaned that Jake is older than Finn by far but often behaves like an immature toddler brat. Although patently irresponsible, this flea-infested creature invokes sarcasm to cheer up his mindless human brother and therefore has, in the Eyes of Evil, a faint modicum of worth.

haha ha!

Jake the Annoying Filth-Dog, as I call him, is stupid, has a very short attention span, and is likely to forget about something immediately after it occurs. For example, rumor has it, he once stuffed an ice-cream cone in a toaster.

I did it on purpose! I wanted the cone toasty!

GET REAL, DUDE.

It is rumored that in times of dire need (or simple laziness), Finn is able to stretch Jake's appendages into absurd new shapes. On one occasion Finn apparently panicked and extended the Filth Dog's ears to avoid touching the ocean, which he inexplicably loathes.

MISCELLANEA CONCERNING THIS PATHETIC DOG

Although it means nothing to me, Jake has saved Finn's life numerous times. He also has Invisible Spiderweb Pants knitted from spiderwebs by Pixies. Moreover, he is apparently semi-magical. For example, I myself have noted that he has magical *Stretchy Powers*, which make him able to stretch his body parts—including internal organs.

Word on the street has it that when Jake was poisoned by an assassin, he immediately enlarged his liver to giant size, enabling it to absorb exceedingly large amounts of toxins so that he would not die. And, unfortunately, he did not.

How did this inane dog develop magical powers? It is said that he got them by rolling around in a magical mud puddle as a puppy, but only a fool would believe that. Let's get past this, shall we, and end with more facts I learned over breakfast from my daughter:

TEN RUMORS CONCERNING JAKE THE DOG

1. Thanks to a wizard's curse, his internal organs apparently smell like vanilla. A hideous and distasteful rumor to be sure.
2. Speaking of smell, he can detect the exact location of any object miles away by odor alone.
3. He is known for his skateboarding skills, banal and worthless as they must be. I can only hope that he will one day jump, ollie, and grind in front of a moving train.

Jake once wrote an unseemly letter to Lady Rainicorn's parents:

"To Mrs. and Mr. Rainicorn, 47 Rainbow St. Please come exactly 1 hour early. I do not have a pet turtle.
—Jake"

4. He is said to be a hideous musician who plays screeching instruments. Rumor has it, his playing Mozart on a viola summoned serpents from the earth. Even worse is his parlor guitar- and ukelele-playing, activities befitting a trendy, innocuous, filthy dog.

5. He speaks Rainicorn and thereby communicates with his unspeakably freakish girlfriend, Lady Rainicorn.

6. To his credit, he is a thief, having snatched old ladies' purses, hocked stolen bikes, and worse. I have been informed that he once hid a bevy of stolen goods under his grotesque rolls of stomach flab.

7. Rumor has it that Jake and Lady Rainicorn once ran naked through a farmer's field. (Technically, however, this rumor is meaningless, since Jake wears spiderweb pants, and Rainicorn is always naked.)

8. Having read his work, I can testify that Jake is a hack journalist and writes a worthless newspaper column titled "Begs the Question."

9. It is said that when you scratch his flea-infested belly, his eyes take on the crazed look of a serial killer and he begins to bark like a tumescent auk during mating season. *AUK AS IN AWK-WARD!!! No way, man!*

There is much more to be said about this dirty, stench-producing canine. But we shall stop here, thankfully shy of Number Ten. For I cannot emphasize enough, O Reader, that the creature in question is merely an insignificant dog who rolls in dirt for pleasure.

Them's fightin' words, Abadeer!

Filthy? I take a bath every day! YEAH, RIGHT!

You tell 'em, Jake!

PRINCESS BUBBLEGUM

PRINCESS BUBBLEGUM

According to Oooian police records, this disgustingly cute creature's full name is Princess Bonnibel Bubblegum, sometimes referred to as "PB" or "Bonnie" or, occasionally, "Peebles." This royal female entity is the ruler of the sickeningly sweet Candy Kingdom.

Princess Bubblegum is a benevolent ruler whose entrancing adorableness repulses all demons of the Nightosphere, including Yours Truly. Her benevolence is so highly refined that she once attempted to revive her dead subjects but, according to my spies, instead accidentally transformed them into a horde of zombie Candy People. She also has a strong love for spaghetti, which she is often seen masticating, munching, and sucking down her grotesque, candy-coated esophagus. *Dad? T.M.I.*

Because of her great beauty and kindness, she is the first creature I shall destroy when at last I conquer the Land of Ooo and enslave its despicable inhabitants. *Get real, Dad. You're not destroying PB.* *Got your back, Marcie!*

Princess Bubblegum is inordinately cultured, highly intelligent, and has an undying passion for science. Why, then, do I find her so detestable? It's quite simple. Her flesh, eyes, hair, and inner organs are made of candy. Sickening enough for you? *DON'T CALL HER MARCIE, DUDE... SHE HATES THAT.*

To her credit, however, Princess Bubblegum occasionally reveals a delightful Dark Side when someone displeases her. For example, my spies report that she has skeletons of past transgressors shackled to her dungeon wall. (Perhaps they mistakenly used one of her combs or ate one of her jellybeans?) *Yeah, to be honest, I wondered about that, too...*

They also inform me that she has, on occasion, shown a modicum of approval to the idea of *torturing* Ice King. But the juiciest report describes how she once pushed the Earl of Lemongrab to the floor, laced his food with hot spices, called him unpleasant names, *and made him cry*!

MUAHAHAHAAAAAAAAAA! I LOVE IT WHEN ADORABLE CREATURES ARE EVIL! Get a grip, pops. Ditto on that!

Excuse me. As I was saying . . . *generally*, when she is in "princess mode," PB is prim, proper, professional, and perfectly poised. If you haven't caught my drift, O Reader, her cuteness and positivity are retchable. But in private with her pals, she apparently loosens up. And Marceline is my Litmus Test of Personality Approvability.

Furthermore, I have heard that the Princess enjoys Finn's company but does not seem to reciprocate his crush on her. (My daughter speculates this may be due to the fact that she is a neat-freak, and Finn once unleashed a pack of wolves in her perfectly appointed room, leaving it in a disreputable state of disarray.) I am also informed that PB gifted Finn with a ghastly pink sweater with a white heart stitched on it. Ugh. I would ask you to kill me now, but unfortunately, I am Deathless.

HER NOXIOUS APPEARANCE

It pains me to describe her putrid cuteness, but my daughter bet me an order of fries that I could not suffer through the writing of this section, and I am loath to lose a wager to my own child. Here we go. PB is a smarmy, pink creature in a pink gown and golden tiara, with hair that is actually made of bubblegum. I know this because I witnessed the witless Tree Witch grabbing a handful and chewing it to prove it really was gum.

Princess Bubblegum, like most of her kind, ignorantly embraces the Post-Human Superstitions known as science, mathematics, and logic, stupidly ignoring the Supreme Art of Nightsopherean Magic. Fancying herself a "scientist," she often prances around in a white lab coat and goggles while performing experiments or working out her inane and boring math equations.

This, unfortunately, brings us to her wardrobe. Since I am a male-gendered demon with impeccable taste, I am utterly disinterested in the pageant of horribly colorful outfits this royal creature sees fit to drape over her turgid candy flesh.

Know this, O Reader, as far as I'm concerned, the only cool thing that Princess Bubblegum ever wore was a black T-shirt given to her by my chic and tasteful daughter, Marceline. Enough said.

Yeah, right, Dad. You've worn the same suit for eight hundred years.

TEN RUMORS CONCERNING THE BUBBLEGUM PRINCESS

1. PB is apparently fluent in German, the preferred language of demons.

2. My records indicate that she's brainy and has a degree in glycomics. (I had to look it up, too.)

3. Security-cam stills show that she keeps a painting of Finn on her wall. (Since I am ignorant of the quaint customs of candy-fleshed creatures, does this mean that she likes him, despises him, or wants to eat him?)

4. Further records show that her closest confidante is the enigmatic sky-fish weirdo, Lady Rainicorn.

5. Police reports have determined she has a pet swan that shoots lasers from its eyes, something which all evil beings can get behind. *Big deal.*

JEALOUS, MARCELINE?

6. I am told she has a "son" named the Earl of Lemongrab whom she created in an imaginative, but botched, science experiment.

No offense, Finn, but PB is actually kind of weird. *TELL ME ABOUT IT, DUDE!*

Although she created Lemongrab to take over the Kingdom in her absence, the Earl is a temperamental ninny whose only desire is to throw everyone, including Princess Bubblegum, in the dungeon.

7. According to my beloved evil daughter, Marceline, PB doesn't like her. To this I say: Fie upon Princess Bubblegum! She shall be the first to be beheaded when my conquest of Ooo is complete! *Dad, quit it! Nobody's beheading anybody.*

8. To her eternal discredit, her BFF is the gargantuan mound of stupidity, Lumpy Space Princess. *You tell 'im, kid!*

9. Rumor also has it that she despises the insufferable Duke of Nuts for eating her pudding, and we of the Nightosphere are all hoping for a violent outcome. *ME, TOO! Me three!*

10. Although the Candy People in her Kingdom will explode if they become overly excited, Princess Bubblegum has repeatedly become excited and *never* exploded. One can only keep hoping . . .

Enough! I tire of enumerating the meaningless minutiae of this pink creature's sickening existence! Moving on!

MARCELINE THE VAMPIRE QUEEN

MARCELINE THE VAMPIRE QUEEN

My exquisitely evil child, Marceline, is my Treasure of Darkness, the hideous Black Rose in the Desiccated Garden of the Nightosphere. My darling dark-haired daughter is more than a thousand years old, but she looks around sixteen. The bad news is she's close friends with Finn the Human and several other ridiculous creatures in the Land of Ooo, scabrous beings of flesh whose souls I will someday suck and whose flesh I shall make into meat pies and feed to their gooning ancestors.

About Marceline's early years: I'm afraid she and I were separated for a short time, mere centuries really, when I had a job that involved a lot of traveling, spreading evil to various far-flung kingdoms. During those years, she and I were separated by an unavoidable Temporal Expanse. Thus, regarding her childhood adventures with her poor, unfortunate mother, there is, now and evermore, naught to be heard but the Shadowfall of Nightospheric Silence.

So, too, about Marceline's reign as Vampire Queen in the Ancient Times of Ooo I will say squat, but about which the Clever Reader may infer much through the misdirected Haze and Umbric Resonance of the Silent Squat I speak. Until the proper time, my lips upon this matter are sealed.

Suffice it to say, I have only love and affection for my Evil Spawn but am incapable of recording the details of her life without the distortion implicit in the love of an evil father for his despicable child. Therefore,

THANKS DAD. THAT'S OUR PRIVATE BUSINESS! Still, it was pretty cool being an actual vampire queen.

I wanna hear all the juicy details. SHUT UP, SHE SAID NO.

I will instead cut and paste various items of interest and whatnot below. After the following interpolations in this, my exquisite Encyclopaedia of the Land of Ooo, I will return to describe the depth and breadth of the remainder of this world in a manner that will astonish the Reader with its insight, alacrity, and astounding brilliance. Brag much, Abadeer?

But for now, there's this:

 **NECKMEAT** NIGHTOSPHERE NETWORKING AGENCY

EXCLUSIVELY REPRESENTING
MARCELINE THE VAMPIRE QUEEN

Dad, the guy who wrote this was a complete moron!

PRESS RELEASE

NECKMEAT NIGHTOSPHERE NETWORKING AGENCY

FOR IMMEDIATE RELEASE!!!

EXCLUSIVELY REPRESENTING

MARCELINE THE VAMPIRE QUEEN!

If you're looking for a cutting-edge, high-visibility vampire about to go viral, *look no further!*

MARCELINE THE VAMPIRE QUEEN is the ultimate high-water mark of red-sucking entertainment! Is your event looking for a demonic singer who plays a bass that was formerly a… bloodstained axe? *Look no further!*

Is your Land of Ooo event light on the proactive, on the sexy, on the sometimes vicious but always lovable undead? Is your event missing a certain songstress who thinks outside the box and comes from Beyond the Pale? *Look no further!*

Spending her time between Uptown Ooo and Downtown Nightosphere, this undead diva, featured in this fall's Bloody Bash 'Zine, has a life story that reads like a guide on how to have maximum face time in the hippest spots in the Ooo Oooniverse!

Thanks to the new digital support of Jake the Dog's number-one column, "Begs the Question," Marceline's life is now the very material of this new medium. Having her hang at your Celebrity Event will put you or your organization at the top of the will-call list of totally immersive pop culture icons!

Always navigating between private sphere and public sphere, Marceline leads her Ooo Entourage through a maze of maximum malevolence that only reveals its surface with opaque elegance! All in all, this vampire vixen brings to the table an autonomous, auto-fictional celebrity fandom, combining bloodthirsty romanticism with the luxurious vibe of demon aesthetics that dazzles the mind with a paradigm shift that we here at **NECKMEAT NIGHTOSPHERE NETWORKING AGENCY** feel exemplifies the cross-channel synergy of a totally organic event-horizon tradigital rep~~~~~~~~~~~~~~~~~~~~bed as a tour de force of

Dad, I hate this! Take it out or I'm burning the rest of it with my plumber's torch.

TEEN ZINE

MARCELINE TELLS ALL!

Can this devilish Diva get a 360 contract?

ice King EXPOSED!
"it's all about my underwear

the Latest Nightosphere Gossip!

EXCLUSIVE
L.O.O. Teen Zine Interview with MARCELINE THE VAMPIRE QUEEN!

TEEN ZINE: *So what's it like to be known as the Diva of Darkness?* **MARCELINE:** Did I actually agree to this interview? What was I thinking? **TEEN ZINE:** *So was there ever a Vampire King?* **MARCELINE:** You realize I could just kill you right now, right? **TEEN ZINE:** *Hahaha!* **MARCELINE:** Shut up. **TEEN ZINE:** *Marceline, word has it you're more than a thousand years old. Does that mean you spend a lot of time on the Internet checking for obituaries and going to friends' funerals? I mean, they must die, like, every week!* **MARCELINE:** How about I arrange yours. Like right now. **TEEN ZINE:** *LOL! I can see now why you're called the Hottie Hater of Hades! Hahaha!* **MARCELINE:** Right. And I completely hate you. **TEEN ZINE:** *Hahahaha!* **MARCELINE:** Shut up. **TEEN ZINE:** *Hahahaha!* **MARCELINE:** Show me your neck. **TEEN ZINE:** *Hahaha—Ow! No! Stop! Gegeuschhh! I thought you didn't—Help! Somebody! Please! For the love of—*

He deserved it!!

MARCELINE'S FAVS & DISSES!

After our editor-in-chief disappeared from our downtown Ooo office, associate editor **Jasmine Honeys** *interviewed Marceline regarding her favs and disses! In her own words:*

MARCELINE'S 3 DISSES

ONE When I was a kid and all alone in the Land of Ooo, I accidentally ran into a pigpen, fell face-first into the mud, and looked up, and this really big hog—out of nowhere—started licking my face. I would've loved it, except that the hog smelled like a filthy sock dipped in sour milk and sprinkled with lint from a fat dude's never-washed belly button. From that moment on, all *PIGS AND HOGS* gave me nightmares. When I dreamed about them, I could still smell them after I woke up. Even writing about them right now brings back that horrible stench. If I could destroy all pigs, I'd probably do it. I'll ask my dad. Maybe he'll suck out all their souls and Ooo will be pigless. Yaay. Second thought: Piglets are kinda cute.

TWO *CELERY.* When I was a little kid and my father forced me to eat his homemade parmesan celery salad, I got a strand of celery gristle stuck in my teeth and couldn't get it out. Not sure why it bugged me so much. But it was definitely one of the worst eating experiences of my life. I wanted to rip my teeth out one by one and throw them into a volcano. Never before had I had a piece of food torture my mouth. If I even see a stalk of celery now, within three seconds I lose my lunch. Gross but true.

THREE *WHEN SOMEBODY EATS MY FRIES.* As you might know, a certain Somebody ate some fries I brought home from the Nightosphere High Corpse-Stretching Contest. I'd been looking forward to those fries all night. So when I caught my Dad eating them without even asking me, I totally freaked. Did I learn something from this? Sure. DON'T EAT MY FREAKIN' FRIES UNLESS YOU WANT A LIFELONG UNDEAD ENEMY!

MARCELINE'S 3 FAVS

ONE *RED FLAGS.* Something about flags makes them cool to suck the red out of. Maybe it's because the creatures in Ooo get all touchy-feely at the sight of a flag, especially a red flag flapping on a flagpole. The red tastes much better on a flapping flag than on any other type of cloth. Maybe the flags somehow gets charged up by the emotions of all the stupid Oooian flag-worshippers. Who knows.

TWO: I really like music in the key of *E FLAT.* Something about that particular vibration sounds really cool to me. I think that's why I like to sing in low keys, because I love singing in E flat. It's the most freakin' awesome key ever created.

THREE: I guess my biggest foodie fav is *FRIES.* I mean, when the lard isn't rancid and doesn't smell like fried chicken and onion rings.

Ten Rumors Concerning Marceline

(Well, in her case they're not rumors; they're all true, but I thought I'd stick to format.)

1. Marceline has a pet zombie poodle named Schwabl.
2. Marceline dumped her boyfriend Ash for selling her prized teddy bear to a witch. She'd named it Hambo, and she had snuggled to sleep with it since she was a kid! Ash was such a jerk!

3. Unlike traditional vampires, Marceline eats the red out of red things, rather than drinking blood. That's fine by me. Blood goes sour after a few minutes, and who likes sour blood? And we all know blood makes a big mess anyhow, so this color red thing is really the way to go.
4. Marceline has a forked tongue she got as a kid when she was chewing gum and accidentally chewed up her tongue. Dad, that's private!
5. As everyone knows, she now has two marks on her neck (see rumor number three), but when I demanded she tell me why, she refused to talk, and we had our first fight to the death. I let her win, but, as she discovered, I am Utterly Unkillable. PSYCH!
Man, she musta been bummed!

I STILL THINK YOUR TONGUE'S COOL! Ewww, gross tongue talk! SHUT IT DAWG!!

6. When Marceline was a child, we discovered she could levitate and float in the air. Even more delightful, when she stands next to someone, she's usually taller, because she can change her form at will.

7. Levitation aside, Marceline's magical powers include pyrokinesis, telekinesis, invisibility, necromancy, shape-shifting (a talent she inherited from Yours Truly), and making me magically delicious pancakes every Father's Day. (As for shape-shifting, she can transform at will into a bat, a wolf, a reptile, or a tentacled monster. Aah, I could not be more proud of my adorable, talented little monster.)

8. Marceline has had lucid dreams whenever she eats tomatoes since she was a child.

9. To my surprise and disappointment, Marceline cannot defeat a ghost. In her own words, "It's like a rock-paper-scissors thing." As her father, I think she should try harder.

10. I am proud to say that my daughter was a prodigy musician as a child and is now a bass player with killer chops. It is also known throughout the Nightosphere that when my daughter sings, everyone is thoroughly entranced and says that she has the exquisite Voice of a Demon.

AWW, LOOKS LIKE POPS LOVES YOU AFTER ALL.   Cool. Thanks Faja.

Cept when they fight to the death. 45

ICE KING

ICE KING

The doddering fool who calls himself Ice King, of course, rules the Ice Kingdom in the Land of Ooo. His Powers allow him to conjure the Absence of Heat and thereby throw ice lightning, transport glaciers via telekinesis, create weird beings out of frozen substances, flash-freeze his enemies, and precipitate malevolent snow, sleet, and hail storms on cue from the mystical core of the nimbostratus.

Ice King's powers are contained in his little crown, without which the insane idiot is powerless.

His crown was apparently the cause of his insanity, as well as the Magical Agency that transformed him into a freakish abomination of flesh, with his goblinic nose, empty white eyes, and long, filthy white beard. I know from experience that when you are in his presence, up close and personal, the stench of his beard alone, unwashed for years at a time, would make an entire herd of alpine yaks heave and retch. Especially avoid him on a day he happens to soil his robes.

I'LL SECOND THAT. HE'S A WALKING OUTHOUSE. Thirded, dude.

Leave him alone, you guys! He can't help being nuts.

{ THE HISTORY OF THE ICE KING }

I have in my possession a VHS copy of a documentary that shows the origin of Ice King and all manner of unpleasantries surrounding the Cloud of his Past. Here is the story of this renowned Idiot of Ooo:

Before the Mushroom War, Ice King was a human named *Simon Petrikov*. Yes, he was an imbecilic human being, a wannabe antiquarian specializing in the study of ancient arcane artifacts.

Petrikov was engaged to be married to a rather bland and banal human female named Betty, whose nickname was "Princess." Through his work, he bought an ancient bejeweled crown that had been discovered frozen in a glacier in Scandinavia. In the worst move of his insignificant life, he brought the ancient crown home, showed it to Betty, and put it on his head to amuse her. But no amusement was to be had.

Instead, the horror began.

When the naïve ninny placed it on his scrawny skull, the crown blasted Petrikov with a surge of powerful, supernatural energy. He shrieked and tried to rip it off his head, but the crown wasn't going anywhere. The jewels began to glow, and Petrikov was engulfed in a swirling cloud of dark energy. His hair turned white! His fingernails turned black and fell off! The pupils of his eyes turned a ghastly, empty white. When Petrikov came to, his beloved Betty fled forever and was never seen again. What happened!? The confused and disoriented flesh-pod had no memory of what he had done or where his beloved had gone. During the transformation, did he somehow scare away his "princess"?

Simon never saw or heard from Betty again, and her disappearance was the beginning of his spiral into despair and a miasma of madness.

Gnashing his teeth and foaming at the mouth, the increasingly insane creature struggled with himself to remove the crown, one hand fighting the other to get it off his head. And when he finally succeeded, he was terrified as he heard hissing voices in a hypnagogic swirl of supernatural visions. His skin turned blue, his nose twisted and elongated like a carrot, his teeth became pointy, and his body temperature plummeted far below that of a normal human.

Major drama bomb... I didn't think you'd put this stuff in here... Wow, Dad.

NO WONDER HE FREAKED OUT AND BECAME SUCH A JERK.

I'm still thinkin' he smells bad.

To his credit, the rapidly cooling dunderhead knew he was losing his mind. So he began to record himself, narrating his quaint story on VHS tape, leaving a record of his bizarre transformation from human moron to demented magical freak.

While he was taping one of these pathetic video diaries, a sudden explosive earthquake rocked his house and rent the earth asunder, cleaving the foundation in twain and crushing the house on its side. He climbed from the rubble, looked to the horizon, and in the distance saw The Horror. The world was filled with explosions that were setting the Land of Ooo aflame from horizon to horizon. The human cretins had succeeded in their program to extinguish themselves from existence, and their insane Mushroom War had begun.

According to the VHS (which I watched while sipping ice-cold lemonade and crunching on tacos), the ancient crown's supernatural power kept Petrikov's flesh from burning in atomic fires. He scrambled hysterically into the burning forest, crawled between two giant rocks, and found an enormous cavern. Once inside, he willed the crown to conjure a blizzard, burying him under a protective blanket of snow and ice.

A Transcript from Petrikov's Pathetic Video Diary

"Hello. My name is Simon Petrikov. I am recording this tape so that people will know my story. I was studying to be an antiquarian of ancient artifacts. Now, I never believed in the supernatural stuff myself, just out of fascination with superstitions. But everything changed when I came into contact with this item.

"After purchasing this crown from an old dockworker in northern Scandinavia, I brought it home and excitedly showed my fiancée, Betty, and jokingly put it on my head just for a laugh or something. And that's

when it started. The visions! I fought with them, shouted at them until I realized none of it was real, it was the crown! I quickly took it off and saw my fiancée in front of me . . . looking at me with such contempt. What had I said? What had I done when I wore this crown? All I know is I never saw Betty again.

"Since then, I now see the visions always, whether or not I wear the crown. They tell me the secrets . . . the secrets of the ice and snow . . . that the power of the crown will save me with its frost. I don't yet know what this means. As you can see, my skin is beginning to turn blue. My body temperature has been dropping at a supernatural rate. I don't know when it will end. I'm really scared.

"I know my mind is changing, but I'm already too far gone to know what to do. I want people to know that . . . if I do things that . . . if I do things that hurt anyone, please, please forgive me.

"Just watch over me until I can find my way out of this laby-rinth in my brain and regain my sanity. And then maybe, Betty, my princess . . . maybe you will love me again. Please love me again, Betty!"

As many years (likely centuries) rolled by, the hibernating fool eventually thawed from a block of ice and revived like a frozen mastodon. Crawling out on all fours, he emerged from the cave to find the once-scarred and blackened landscape transformed. It was now alive and flourishing with green plant life covering the ancient, charred ruins.

However, he was now quite mad. Petrikov was gone, and in his place was Ice King, growing more insane every day. But knowledge of his original identity was still buried somewhere in his subconscious by the supernatural power of the ice crown. A piece of Petrikov's personality still affected Ice King and created in him a strange and desperate desire to marry a "Princess." And now, lonely and grouchy, Ice King spends his days kidnapping and imprisoning the various Princesses of Ooo, without knowing why.

Awww. Wow, I'm tearing up, Dad. He couldn't help what happened. I always felt bad for him. ☺ LIFE'S TOUGH. BUT I STILL DON'T WANNA HANG W/ THE GUY.

TEN RUMORS CONCERNING ICE KING

Ditto.
A jerk's
a jerk.

1. I admit that the senile fool is a passable musician. He practices drum solos and plays keyboards and other instruments strewn about his castle. (Although I hear they've jammed together, nothing this fool plays compares to the evil musicianship of my lovely daughter.)

2. His filthy, horrible-smelling beard has magical powers of its own. It can move like an appendage, shapeshift into a weapon, or sprout wings that allow him to fly—although he resembles a senile nincompoop when he flies in this absurd manner.

3. My sources tell me that the insane king brags about being a master of the Ice Ninja art of Fridjitzu but in reality often knocks himself out with his own pair of nunchakus.

4. When he shaves off his beard, he behaves so differently that people call him the "Nice King."

5. Ice King has a tattoo of a penguin on his butt, which, common sense dictates, is better left forever unseen.

6. Symptomatic of his demented confusion, Ice King once accidentally married Jake.

7. Like many Oooian fools, Ice King is addicted to video games, and his favorite game is *Battle Babe*.

8. One of Ice King's most lurid hobbies is to fill his bathtub with milk and take a bath while imagining that he's a magical angel floating through the Milky Way.

9. Sources say he often falls asleep with his eyes open, a sight that creeps out the most black-hearted villain.

10. A strange rumor circulating through the Land of Ooo states that Ice King wears a golden locket with pictures of two people inside—Finn and Jake. I leave you, O Reader, to draw your own hideous conclusions.

LADY RAINICORN

LADY RAINICORN

This freakish female behemoth is known as Lady Rainicorn. She is a bizarre, hybrid creature—half unicorn, half rainbow—and Princess Bubblegum's friend and companion. She resides in a filthy stable in the Cotton Candy Forest and occasionally tags along during Finn and Jake's questionable adventures.

Distastefully, she is also Jake's main squeeze and the mom to his pups. The mind reels. *Back off, Abadeer! That's my GIRL!!!*

Inexplicably, Lady Rainicorn speaks a pre–Mushroom War language known as Korean but can communicate in English using a mechanical Universal Translator. (The Translator is limited to three Speech Modes: *Old Man*, *Nerdy Alien*, and *Nightmare*.)

My sources inform me that this bizarre creature can fly because when her body intercepts light beams it can "dance around" on them. She can also fly through walls by instantly altering the molecular structure of her body and the molecular structure of anyone riding her, allowing both to pass through solid objects.

The flying Beast can use her unicorn horn to change the color of any object. And randomly, like Jake, she plays the viola. Since the freak possesses only fingerless hooves, my guess on one word to describe her playing? Horrendous.

HER APPEARANCE

Yet another hideously cute creature of the Land of Ooo, this weird talking sky-snake has rainbow-colored stripes along her serpentine body, a blond equine mane, and what I infer to be a deadly pointed horn, useful in a pinch as a mortal weapon.

Finn, better not let Jake read this part.

I'M ON IT. I ALREADY DISTRACTED HIM WITH A CUCUMBER SANDWICH.

TEN RUMORS CONCERNING LADY RAINICORN

Lay off, Abadeer! Rainy's not half as freaky as you are!

RIGHTEOUS COMEBACK DUDE!

1. Prepare to recoil with disgust: It is rumored that this female freak and the filth-dog Jake play a game called Seven Minutes in Heaven, in which they are locked in a closet together to kiss for seven minutes. Ugh.

2. One of my demon spies has informed me that the crumbling fool Mr. Cupcake has a crush on the colorful freak in question.

3. My daughter told me that when she saw Jake and Rainicorn seated together at the movies, ~~they spent the~~ ~~~~ ~~~~ ~~~~ ~~~~ ~~~~ ~~~~ ~~~~ ~~~~ ~~macking?~~

DAD! I said thought they were ~~~~

*Dude, we were just **talking**!!*

4. According to security-cam freeze-frames obtained through the Oooian Freedom of Information Act, Princess Bubblegum has two pictures of Lady Rainicorn in her castle, one of her upper half and one of her lower half.

5. The Sky Snake and Jake had five pups: Charlie, T.V., Viola, Kim Kil Whan, and Jake Jr. These puling brats grew to adulthood in a few hours. One can only imagine the splendor of changing five sets of oopy diapers.

6. Though she appears cute and adorable, the creature in question is more than capable of kicking butt in a fight. My sources reveal she actually saved Finn from an underwater beating by the soggy morons known as Lake Knights. YEOWCH! STILL GOT THE GASH TO PROVE IT.

7. According to a stolen dossier in my possession, the Sky Monster's favorite drink is iced latte with no whipped cream.

8. Yuck! Rumor has it that the female Beast taught Jake how to cook Korean food, the least favorite food of demons.

9. Concerning the disturbingly cute progeny of Rainicorn and Jake the dog, the less said the better. I cannot abide the happiness of others, especially if it involves that detestable filth-dog.

10. Her physical anomaly has been noted: Although her body contains all other colors of the rainbow, it does *not* contain any orange. I ask, O Demon Reader, in implicit tones of sarcasm: Will the Mysteries of Ooo never end?

LUMPY SPACE PRINCESS

LUMPY SPACE PRINCESS

I, Hunson Abadeer, Lord of the Evil Domain of the Nightosphere, personally despise this ghastly, bulbous creature. Though I cringe with distaste, I begin: Lumpy Space Princess (or LSP), or rather, the Princess of Repulsiveness, dwells in the bleary, aetheric realm of Lumpy Space, a Nether Region of the Land of Ooo known for producing creatures even more moronic than the Inhabitants of Ooo. Lumpy Space Princess is yet another sky freak, having no legs, and manages to get around by floating. A quick check of police records shows that, like a werewolf or vampire, if she or others of the Lumpy Kind bite non-lumpy beings, she can infect them with "The Lumps."

This most disgustingly shallow and most worthless of all Oooian Princesses resembles a bulbous, purple pile of ooze regurgitated by a dog. My sources tell me, however, that this creature is actually composed of irradiated stardust. Hardly believable, but I'll give them the benefit of the doubt. LSP has a strangely masculine voice, as if dubbed by a bearded intellectual man mocking her babbling inanity from another dimension. Like her royal parents, she has a yellow star on her forehead that glows as she floats mindlessly hither and thither. Sources say that she appears to have an unpleasant layer of short, hairy fuzz all over her body, much like

the molting fur of an immature swamp sloth. Hairy, bulbous, shallow, lumpy—I ask you, can a being be any more putrid?

My spies tell me that LSP's blithering, imbecilic friend Melissa dates a lumpy boy named Brad, who is LSP's ex-boyfriend. As one might expect, this shallow triangle of despair inspires a plethora of vapid high school drama, and we are regaled by boring, repetitive, contentless stories about Brad and LSP hitting the drive-through and arguing while eating chili cheese fries together.

By all accounts, LSP is disinterested in anything but her own revolting essence. Her speech is characterized by endless, sing-songy, superficial chattering. My spies say she is quick to dismiss others with mindless catchphrases, such as "*WhatEVER*" and "*Lump OFF.*"

From my spies: Although this royal pile of ooze often loses her temper and insults people, she has actually credited Finn and Jake as "real friends" as opposed to her "fake" high school friends.

YEAH, SHE'S OK, JUST A LITTLE ON THE LAME SIDE.

I think she's cute. PSYCH!

Pops got his harsh on today.

TEN RUMORS CONCERNING LUMPY SPACE PRINCESS

1. It is reported that when she ran away from home and camped in the woods, her favorite hobo food was "Full O' Bean" brand beans.
2. Intel I've received suggests that another filthy pile of princess meat called Turtle Princess is one of her best friends.
3. I have been supplied with photographic proof that LSP is able to barf rainbows. *Blecchh!!*
4. Forgive me for the obvious padding of this, the most dubious portion of my Encyclopaedia, when I say her choice of esophageal lubrication appears to be diet soda.

5. Although the Princess in question obviously sickens me, I, Hunson Abadeer, Lord of Evil and Imperator of the Entire Nightosphere Kingdom, offer the strange admission: Lumpy Space Princess haunts my dreams, appearing in them as the most exquisite creature in the universe. Why this preposterous creature should appear to me as a wondrous paragon of perfection during sleep, I have no idea, but I am seeing a shrink about it.

Dad, are you OK?

Are you allergic to that new sinus medicine you're taking?

6. According to my demon spies, she is the worst girlfriend in the History of Ooo. Example? She broke up with her boyfriend Brad immediately after he kissed her on the mouth, whining that she "wasn't ready."

Somebody kissed THAT mouth?!

7. I will add in deference to the protocol of Full Disclosure that when she appears in my dreams, LSP demonstrates an ethereal, magnificent, operatic singing voice, the vibratory tones of which (in my dreams) make me weep into my manicured claws. *Don't go there, Dad.*

Feeling weird. Stomach. Queasy. Vomit rising.

8. A security dossier suggests that she invited Finn and Jake to her quinceañera celebration, and later served as their secretary, for the sole purpose of digging up dirt for a backstabbing, trashy tell-all book for ladies. Surprisingly evil for such a mindless and obnoxious blob!

9. It is speculated that one could become infected by LSP's strangely sharp set of canine teeth. *It totes happened to me!*

10. Due to an utter lack of interest in her repugnant character, I refused to contribute any more to the odious subject. I hereby expunge and erase any further thoughts of the Princess in question from this Book.

One moment. I take that back. To inject novelty into this horrid section of my otherwise Magnificent Encyclopaedia, I shall now vary this presentation for the aesthetic relief of my Readers and thereby entertain while educating. Since this dull, hapless blob is in reality a bona fide Princess, and her life reads somewhat like a fairy tale, I shall now conjure her pathetic drama in full storybook mode:

YEAH, CHECK THE EXPIRATION DATE, DUDE.

The Tale of The
LUMPIEST PRINCESS
There Ever Was

ONCE UPON A TIME, LSP, as she is sometimes called, had an argument with her parents, the eponymous Lumpy Space Queen and King, about going to the Promcoming Dance. As a result, our Lumpy Heroine ran away from home through a secret portal to the delightful Land of Ooo.

There she lived like a homeless vagabond along the highways and byways, unwashed, stinking, and lonely, living in a hobo tent where she cooked cans of beans and meaty roadkill over a campfire. Yum!

Seeking shelter from a terrible storm, Her Lumpiness was taken in and adopted by a family of wolves. She lived with them happily for a time, despite her teen angst, communicating with them via hand signs and body language.

Then, one fateful day, our now filthy and animalistic Princess happened upon a girl wolf cheating on her boyfriend wolf with another boy wolf. Our stinking heroine was furious, since the girl wolf's boyfriend was her wolf brother. In truth, the boy and girl wolves were merely cleaning each other with their tongues, but LSP overreacted and slapped the girl wolf!

Bad move! Wolves hate that! The entire pack turned on her, chasing her in a fury of claws, gnashing teeth, and flying threads of saliva! Terrified and disoriented, Her Royal Lumpiness was chased to the end of a rocky precipice and, screaming, fell off the edge! Oh, no!

Losing consciousness, our poor, stinking purple heroine rolled down the mountainside, splashing through puddles, crashing through bushes, tumbling through mud pits, getting even more filthy. When she awoke, tired, sweaty, crusted with mud and brambles, she found herself lying at the edge of a field of tasty crops beside a small village.

The villagers took one look at her and were shocked. They mistook her weird, filthy carcass for a monster and ran away screaming. Oh, no!

Safe from the wolves and quite hungry, Lumpy Space Princess began to chow down on the crops in the field. Eat, eat, eat! The villagers tried to stop her, but the wild-eyed princess belched and grunted, stuffing her face, terrorizing the villagers so she could keep eating their crops without them bothering her.

Meanwhile, her parents asked the great Oooian heroes, Finn the Human and Jake the Dog, to find their Lost Princess and bring her home. Finn and Jake endured many awesome adventures and finally found her in the field, making crop sandwiches and stuffing her face.

Finn and Jake suggested that she apologize
to the villagers so they'd cool down. LSP agreed, and tried to
apologize to the villagers. But her teen angst got in the way,
and she ended up getting in an argument with them
and called the villagers fat!

Furious, the villagers formed a mob and
tried to kill her, screaming that they needed the crops to feed
their children. Hearing this, Lumpy Space Princess had an epiphany:
Her Royal Lumpiness realized that she truly cared for and needed
her parents, mainly because they would feed her with no hassles,
and she returned home to live out her days happily,
and lumpily, forever after.

THE END

II

UTTERLY INSIGNIFICANT INHABITANTS OF THE LAND OF OOO

WHOM I YEARN to DESTROY

Within the noxious realm of the Nightosphere, over which I reign supreme, all Beings save Myself may be considered Secondary Creatures. It's neat and simple. But in the Land of Ooo, a lowerarchy of Utterly Insignificant Beings exists, whose mere presence on the planet is a personal irritation to my refined sensibilities.

But since I promised my daughter that this Encyclopaedia would offer a comprehensive survey of All Things Ooooian, I will now use Evil Psychic Resonance, as well as intel received from spies, informers, and other shadowy sources. To tell the truth, since I despise actual research, I shall mostly be riffing by glancing at their obnoxious likenesses that pollute the following pages. Here, then, are the Least Interesting Fools and Wastrels of Ooo, in all of their post-Byzantine glory.[6]

Abraham Lincoln A bearded human nincompoop so obnoxiously clingy to life that he refused to die, took up residence on the Planet Mars, and there became King. Symptomatic of His Stupidity, Lincoln sacrificed himself to save the one Oooian creature who annoys me most—Jake the Filth-Dog.

Abracadaniel Although I am most fortunate not to know him, I am told this so-called wizard wastes his time transforming things into butterflies and rainbows. For this I hereby pledge to suck out his obscuris spiritus at my first opportunity.

Aquandrius A devious, mud-slathered labyrinth serpent, admirable in his enthusiastic desire to do evil through the use of craftily granted wishes. However, after this amateur of evil tactlessly defeated me in a Slithering Contest, I ordered my guards to remove and shellac his eyeballs for use in a game of bocce.

WHAT'S BOCCE?

who cares? My turn to doodle, dewd.

Ash My daughter's pathetic ex-boy-friend and a Stain upon the Landscape of Ooo. I have compiled and now present a telling clipping regarding this shiftless imbecile. From *The Candy Kingdom Dispatch*:

WHAT'S NEW IN OOO?

The controversial, wannabe-wizard known as "Ash" was arrested today for the alleged crimes of Fencing Stolen Property, Impersonating a Wizard under the fake name "Rag Wizard," Stealing Memories, and for Being a General Pain in the Butt. The defendant Ash told this reporter that there wasn't a jail cell in Ooo that could stop him from

Talk about a MORON!!

BMO (Beemo) According to security reports from my demon spies, BMO is Finn and Jake's sentient and mobile computer—also their handy-man and roomie, programmed with a simulated personality. It is clear that this creature does not exist, for it is not even *alive*. This machine is obviously genderless and is referred to as It in its worthless instructional pamphlet, which I have included for reference on page 109.

Banana Man Although I have never met this fruit-based simpleton, I know by his picture that one day the trajectory of my phlegm is destined to intersect with the spittoon of his face.

Bufo Raise your hand if the mere thought of tadpoles wearing small wizard hats and living inside a toad makes you physically ill. (*All hands in the universe raise.*) Yes, I am being cute, but with good reason. After my eventual invasion of the Land of Ooo, if they are lucky, I will let these indecorous, slimy beings rot in a bottomless filth-hole of despair.

Balloon Creatures Rubbery, inflatable beings whose obnoxiousness is the Stuff of Legends. On a positive note, they explode to death.

Banana Guards An embarrassing species that should be fed with great enthusiasm to baboons harboring communicable mouth diseases.

Bellamy Bug My daughter returned my query about this creature with the following inexplicable text: "Finn said he made him beat himself up. Then he thinks some penguins ate him." My daughter would never lie. Therefore, she's obviously gone completely insane. Dad, Knock it off.

THAT BUG ENDED UP W/ A ROBOT ARM AND AN OCTOPUS TENTACLE!!

Don't bother, dude.

Billy Finn and Jake's "idol," reputed to be Ooo's greatest hero. But in reality, Billy is an over-the-hill, crapulous cretin, now hired by villagers out of pity as a handyman, pizza deliverer, or scarecrow. According to my despicable demon spies, a list of his repulsive, goodie-goodie deeds would include:

a) rescuing Cotton Candy Princess from the Fire Count.

b) slaying an ocean.

c) defeating a giant bear.

d) facing off with an Evil Rival of mine who shall remain Nameless, a Dolt of Darkness upon whom I may rant later.

Thankfully, this mindless thrill junkie's glory days are over. Behold the remains

Hey, OK if I start doodling again?

GO FOR IT.

of Ooo's greatest hero, O Reader, now a sagging, wrinkled bag of malodorous flesh, soon to be brunch for worms.

SEZ YOU, BONEHEAD!

Yeah! What he said!

Blastronaut A cut-rate robotic assassin who is actually a mechanical tin can operated by a stinking gnome. Good riddance to bad rubbish.

Boilbee An inept evil ghost with a stupid name whose grave, after the Invasion, I shall relocate to a bowling alley Dumpster.

Boobafina A female duck who, instead of staining the pages of my Encyclopaedia, would be better served slathered with hot sauce and skewered over a Nightosphere barbecue. Are you irritated that this entry has no informational content whatsoever? Boohoo.

Booboo An empty-headed specter (and chum of my daughter Marceline's) who has two mouths, thereby making him twice as annoying.

Breakfast People Edible inhabitants of the cholesterolic Breakfast Kingdom, ruled by their horrible-tasting rulers, Breakfast Princess and Toast Princess. Question: Upon waking, do they eat themselves?

Businessmen A horde of formally attired zombies who, like all businesspeople, are detail-oriented dunces. Word has it they are survivors of the ancient Mushroom War and were frozen centuries ago in an iceberg. Rumors that the idiots Finn and Jake thawed and used them as dockworkers are as yet unsubstantiated. I Myself recently hired them as parking valets for the annual Nightosphere Bingo Bash and paid them with the rancid gore of a rotting dingo.

Butterfly Bandit Sources say that this lowlife lepidoptera pirated poisoned pastries, an alliterative but insignificant act that My Readers are now wasting their time reading about.

Choose Goose An obnoxious and chatty fowl who, for his gift of speaking in rhyme, I nominate for Immediate Execution. Gaze upon his visage, O Reader, and tell me honestly if he should not be instantly fried in oil and fed to a family of ferrets.

Cactus Creatures A lowly race of thorny plant beings inhabiting the Deserts of Ooo, or so I am told. On occasion they are known to bother passersby by their mere existence.

Candy People One of the signature mutations in Oooian life-forms is sentient candy and foodstuffs. Presumably a side effect of radiation from the ancient Mushroom War, Candy People inhabit the sickeningly cute environs of the Candy Kingdom. Leading Candy People include Mr. Candy Cane, Mr. Cream Puff, and Mr. Cupcake.

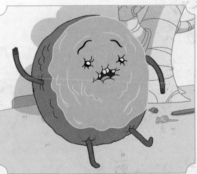

What a weirdo...

Cinnamon Bun A donut-shaped citizen who eschews pants in order to show off his cinnamon buns. Why do I allow creatures like this to live? This is a philosophical question, O Reader, unworthy of its pantless subject matter. Moving on!

THE BEST THING ABOUT BUNS IS THE HOLE IN HIS HEAD.

Hey, what's "eschews" mean?

Clown Nurses A race of rancid, painted beings who are allergic to the organ of intelligence.

Cuber A freakish phantasm I once hired to host a Halloween Sugar Rush Party. (I just e-mailed myself a reminder to hire him as host of our next Execution Fun Festival and Intestines Raffle.)

Cute King I met the irrepressible Cute King at last year's Evilcon when he was Guest Speaker on my panel "Is Killing Ghosts Murder?" Cute King leads the inane race of Cuties, who have childlike voices and adorable exoskeletons. His quaint homicidal tendencies and dreams of Burning Down the Universe have made him a singularly popular guest at "Bring Your-Own-Corpse" Cocktail Parties.

Death The drummer in my first cover band, whom I kicked out of the group for being better than me. Since he was a good buddy, it is regrettable that I must destroy him to maintain my sovereignty as His Badness Numero Uno. _This guy Rocks!!_

Donny From secretly reading Marceline's e-mails, I learned of this obnoxious plant ogre who was once roommates with Finn and Jake. However, their roomie experience soon backfired. I'd go on, but writing even this much about Donny transports me into a somnambulant stupor.

Door Lord A troublesome supernatural creature portal guardian whose absurd appearance makes me wonder if I imagined him into existence after eating some bad Indian food.

Dr. Dextrose A marshmallow creature employed as a scientist by Bubblegum Princess. I can only dream of skewering his gooey flesh on a stick over an open flame.

Dr. Ice Cream The personal physician of Princess Bubblegum, whose brave attempts to keep her alive should be rewarded with red-hot skewers thrust through her eye sockets, repeatedly, and with gusto. Any questions? No? Excellent!

Dr. J The Candy Kingdom Police Blotter lists this deformed waffle-cone as head of a gang of diamond thieves. If you are evil and in need of stolen goods, Dr. J is the bomb.

Duke, Duchess, and Marquis of Nuts A squalid royal family composed of permutations on the concept of "nut people." Their second son, even less notable than the rest, I shall not even deign to mention here. Since none of them are of any consequence in the Scheme of Things, pass me a nutcracker, O Reader, so that I may snack upon their essence while I watch the game.

Eberhardt While evilly perusing my daughter's secret diary while she was away at the movies, I learned that she sucked the color red from this brainless boob's necktie. I admit I wept fulsomely with pride, and it was my tears drenching her diary pages that, upon her return, ratted me out.

Earl of Lemongrab This sentient, high-strung lemon creature was created in a bioengineering experiment by Princess Bubblegum. Since Lemongrab was technically PB's son, and yet was somehow *older* than her, he tried to take over the Kingdom but proved to be an incompetent nincompoop whose soul begs me to suck it. Do you, O Reader, sense that for the crime of manifesting this Stain upon Existence, the Universe should be given a time-out?

Ed and Barb While skimming *Arachnid Monthly*, I came across Finn's name in a relationship profile of Ed and Barb, a pedestrian giant spider couple. I would be happy to relate its contents to you, My Unholy Readers, had I not ripped the article to shreds and fed it to filth-goats. *C'est la mort.*

Flambo A despicable snitch in the shape of a living campfire who gives up information on Ice King's various kidnapping schemes. When Flambo's tips are especially juicy, Finn tosses him a piece of charcoal, which Flambo gobbles up like the lowly dog that he is.

Fear Feaster I blanch to convey the disgusting story of the Feast Creature, which I heard thirdhand while giddy on strawberry milkshakes at a poker game. It seems that when Finn the Human first experienced Extreme Mortal Fear, a rather unpleasant, tornado-shaped psycho-creature emerged from his intestines. A bizarre and baffling battle ensued between the two. This resulted in Finn banishing the Fear Feaster back into the depths of his bowels. Here's my card. Call me the next time you want to be repulsed.

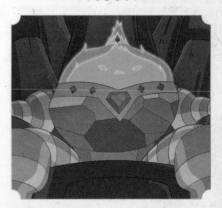

Flame King My colleague in evil, although lightweight compared to the Iron Hand with which I rule the Nightosphere. If he ever gives me the slightest guff, I shall blow him out like a three-year-old's birthday cupcake. (Did I mention I despise him?)

Forest Cyclops I have had the displeasure of observing this foul-smelling giant cowering in fear in the Oooian forests and learned that his wimpy tears have magical healing powers as well as the ability to bring an inanimate object, such as a ham sandwich, to life. In addition, his head can detach from his body, which will undoubtably come in handy when I eventually decapitate him to rid myself of his unspeakable Cyclopsian stench.

Forest Wizard I have decapitated this Wizard not three, not four, not five, but six times, but his annoying wife keeps sewing his head back on. Yet each time, his neckhole gushes gore with great excitement, as if his inner effluents are embarrassed and desperate to escape from within such a self-evident imbecile.

Georgy A ghostly acquaintance of my daughter who almost killed Finn and Jake dead. Although this makes me like her, Marceline intimated that Georgy should be peremptorily destroyed. *Dad, I was kidding!*

NO. SHE WASN'T. I DARE YA!

Dude! Double-dare!

Gnomes I am familiar with this race of pugnacious creatures who inhabit the Beneathaverse Kingdom. Three in number, the Gnomes have one singularly redeeming quality: They enthusiastically destroy feeble Elderly Ladies. What's not to like?

Gnome Ruler Nicknamed by demon children "The Boob of Beneathaverse," this cretinous, white-bearded ninny canceled out whatever street cred he had accrued when he mouthed the words "sexy fun dancing." For this verbal infraction, the Gnome Ruler's soul, such as it is, will be sucked unceremoniously from his unseemly, miniature flesh-bag of gore, and spat into a restroom receptacle frequented by fetid, malodorous Butt Creatures.

Goliad A gooey quadruped clone created by Princess Bubblegum as an heiress to her kingdom. However, Goliad soon focused her puny psychic energy on destroying PB and—oh, I must have drifted off. Ho-hum. Is there a drearier tale of dullness in existence, O Demon Reader? The answer: No.

Grob Gob Glob Grod Although the details are a tad sketchy, sources indicate that this four-faced Martian is very difficult to videochat with. Not to mention a confusion arises, since each face has an absurdly similar name. GGGG did, however, come to my palace one night, and we played charades and he made excellent fudge brownies.

HER BORING SIDE

THE SIDE I DESIRE

Guardian Angel If I was forced with a blunderbuss to the sternum to name a monster I love, the name of this creature would surely croak from my trembling lips. If I invited myself over to her place for dinner, I understand that Finn and Jake might be the main course. What could make for a more satisfying meal?

Gummy I blanch to admit that occasionally this lowly goblin weasels his way into our Thursday Texas Hold'em Poker Nights. His obnoxious insistence on following the precise rules and on chewing our food for us drove us to use the Spell of Mahendra to banish him to the interior of a porcelain toilet I saw abandoned in front of a trailer park.

that I had met my match. Gunter's Black Qualities are the most exquisitely formidable in the Galaxy and include stealing change from blind blues harmonica players and hatching a floating pink kitten.

HE HATCHED A KITTEN!!!

Gunter This is the fearsome name of Ice King's chief penguin, the most Incredibly Evil Creature I have ever encountered. Yes, O Lovers of Evil, I *did* try to suck out its soul, but soon found

Hot Dog People A race of beings whose kingdom inexplicably consists of a small patch of grass with a doghouse and a fence around it. Or perhaps I dreamed that. In either case, after my Invasion of Ooo, they will be among the first race my demon armies devour whole, once our mustard supplies arrive.

I STILL DON'T KNOW IF GUNTER'S A GUY OR A GIRL.

Dude. Stop thinking or your brain will explode.

Hug Wolves Marceline claims Finn was once hugged by a member of this hug-craving race and that the hug transformed Finn into a horrible Hug Wolf himself. I ask you, how can that which is horrible *become* horrible?

Faja, that's just stupid!

Jelly Bean People O Demon Reader, know that in the insane asylum called the Land of Ooo, walking and talking jelly beans operate a bakery and make hard-crusted pastries. I am speaking of the abomination known as *Tarts*. My hatred of these inedible wheat excretions is second only to the race that makes them—Jelly Bean People.

Jaybird A candy cane thug I might possibly vote for in an election for the position of Chief Loser of Moronville. He is a notorious simpleton and, not surprisingly, an enthusiastic male model for sugar-cone dunce caps. Let us enthusiastically hate him together, O Demon Reader.

Jermaine An Insignificant Canine Creature, Jake's brother, and the most boring filth-dog ever created in the history of the world. Shall we move on? Yes, we shall.

Jiggler Marceline adopted one of these inane, barbellish creatures as a pet. Whenever she is away, however, I use this worthless creature as nature intended, as a doorstop, footrest, doggie toy, bathtub plug, or something to jam in a window to keep it open. Thus ends my muted diatribe regarding this zero composed of emptiness wrapped in a nothing.

Joshua and Margaret Jake the Filth-Dog's smarmy parents, whose mere presence in this book makes me retch due to their tedious and insufferable cuteness. (See *Jake*.)

Yaaay! Mom and Pop made it in a book!!

Key-per A Door Lord–like freakazoid, having a key on his head instead of a door. In truth, the Key-per does not have the key; the Key-per *is* the key. Know, O Demon Reader, that on occasion I dream of this absurd creature after a meal of soda crackers and Hungarian Goulash.

The Lich The only thing I abhor more than a being Better than Myself is a being Worse than Myself. Such a being is the detestable Lich. He is my only real rival in the race for invading and plundering the World of Ooo. Although The Lich's army of undead skeletal knights is a tad on the pathetic side, I believe they are yet capable of destroying Ooo utterly, and thus I take his presence as My Rival seriously. I would take him even *more* seriously if he were a snappy sartorialist. For example, in the above picture, he's wearing black socks with sandals under his dress. Or is it a kaftan? You catch my drift.

However, O Demon Reader, since The Lich was roundly defeated by the ultimate annoying Ooooian—Finn the Human—what is stopping me from wiping the floor with old skull head and then using what's left over as rags to wash and wax my vintage '78 Camaro? The answer, I admit, is my own indolence and mental otiosity, a condition for which I am presently seeing a shrink.

Lumpy Space People A dim-witted species of Purple Cloud Beings who, having no skull, therefore have no repository for a brain. Somewhat vampiric in nature, their bite transforms hapless victims into lumpy igno-ramuses. Although I have promised not to mention her again, a certain tawdry Princess of this Kingdom visits my dreams, haunting my slumber as a wraith of wonderment.

Lumpy Space King and Queen According to Marceline, Lumpy Space Princess's parents, who, like all Lumpy married people, are physically fused together. As a result, Divorce is unpopular in the Lumpy Space Realm due to the deafening shrieks when husband and wife are physically ripped apart. If any professional assassins are reading, please feel free to destroy these idiotic creatures whose regrettable existence is a Stain upon the Skein of the Nigh-tospherean Universe.

MY MOST HATED WIZARDS OF OOO

A BRIEF GLOSSARY

OF EVEN MORE INSIGNIFICANT BEINGS BY HUNSON ABADEER, LORD OF EVIL

ABRACADANIEL

Repeated mention of this moron makes me yearn for a cosmic clam knife with which to disgorge the universe.

ASH

Yes, I've discussed my daughter's ex-boyfriend sorcerer elsewhere. Arrested for being Ugly and Stupid, he relied on primitive and lame magic.

DIMENSION WIZARD

A four-armed, pink-eyed triclops who can open portals between dimensions. A real hunk to female demons, I hear.

FOREST WIZARD

A delightfully vengeful guardian of the forest and all its creatures.

GRAND MASTER WIZARD

This master of wizard ceremonies oversees the Wizard Battle and is, unfortunately, a fan of filthy felines.

ICE KING

Enough has been blathered about this Ice Cube Clown already, has it not?

NAKED WIZARD

A white-bearded imbecile who cannot stand clothing, and whose naked state embarrasses the universe.

ROCK WIZARD

A levitating paleo-sorcerer capable of summoning meteor showers and rebuilding himself when broken apart by opponents. Any questions?

ULTIMATE WIZARD

The highest class of wizardry, attained only by wizards who either performed the feats necessary to acquire every magical power or bribed an official to sign their Ultimate Wizard Certificate.

WIZARD THIEF

An old wizard in the City of Thieves with the pathetic ability to transform into a cat. You call that a wizard?!

Magic Man A rather unfocused entity from Mars who disguises himself as a jolly, homeless hobo and travels from town to town seeking a cup of water, a few crackers, and the complete subjugation of all life on Ooo. **I HATE HIM.** Ditto.

Me-Mow Although she belongs to a race of cute, fluffy parasites that Oooian freaks called *pets*, Me-Mow aspires to be a full-fledged killer in the Guild of Assassins. Activities to her credit include:

a) the unfortunately fruitless assassination attempt on Wildberry Princess.

b) illegally hiding in Jake's nose until he agreed to kill the Princess.

c) eluding capture by flying away on the back of a bluebird.

Note to Self: On an artistic level, Me-Mow's appearance seems primitive, almost as if a child had designed her. But I digress.

Mildwin A lugubrious slime creature and leader of the Moldos, a race of slugs infesting Turtle Princess's library. *Warning: If you stupidly devour Mildwin or any of his ilk, a bitter aftertaste will linger in your gullet for weeks. To clear the pallet, I recommend gargling with nuclear plasma and scraping the throat canal with a garden trowel, followed by a breath mint.*

Mini Queen A clingy, mindless insect Queen who, Marceline informs me, has a crush on Finn, despite the fact he's roughly eight thousand times her size. Since her voice is too soft to be heard, she scrawls moronic messages on Finn's hand, such as "XOXO CALL ME."

Dude, you have such weird chicks crushing on you. GO CHEW ON A DOGGIE TOY.

The Morrow Princess Bubble-gum's giant pet falcon on which she flies to the Grocery Kingdom. Candy Kingdom lawyers have their hands full covering up hundreds of deaths, victims of falling falcon poo.

Mountain Man A living ~~JAKE~~ mountain who is oversensitive to violence and whines and sobs when he sees grown men fighting. Ironically, his tears fall as giant boulders, which crush villagers by the hundreds.

~~JAKE~~ ~~JAAAKE~~ ~~Jake~~

Mutants The Land of Ooo is ~~JAKE~~ crawling with mutants created by nuclear radiation from the Mushroom War. Prominent mutant races and individuals include Hyoomens, Candy People, inhabitants of Freak City, and individuals such as Princess Bubble-gum, Princess Princess Princess, Penny, Old Man Henchman, Evil Monster, and other assorted freaks infesting the Land of Ooo.

Never-Ending Pie-Throwing Robot (Neptr) This absurd contraption was built by Finn to throw pies at Jake. But when it was hit by lightning, the robot came to life. Thinking that even more lightning would fully charge it, Finn took Neptr to Ice King's palace to fight, hoping Ice King would blast the machine with lightning bolts. The plan worked, but Ice King's electricity unexpectedly gave Neptr an obsessive desire to collect Princesses. I ask you, Reader, will this pathetic melodrama never end?

Finn, do I have good handwriting for a dog? Just wondering.

YOU MEAN PAW-WRITING?? IT'S AWESOME. I DON'T KNOW HOW YOU CAN DRAW SO GOOD WITH NO OPPOSABLE THUMB. I know, it's weird!

Paper Pete A small, folded paper creature and leader of the Pagelings, who inhabit Turtle Princess's Library. My only experience with this dull creature was using him to wrap carp at the Nightosphere Rotted Fish Market.

Party Pat In the history of all the bears and bear-like creatures that have ever existed in the Land of Ooo, none deserves his soul sucked from his carcass with zest and alacrity more than this odious, fuzzy-wuzzy, Party Animal of Tedium. His contrived, low-key exuberance is the precise quality which I most abhor in sentient creatures, combined with the fact that

I despise the wretched race of bears. May I remember to conjure Party Pat to party on to Eternity upon the Empty Karaoke Stage of Utter Oblivion.

Party God The only Oooian god who is not a smarmy, smug fool. Delightfully rude and ill-mannered, Party God resembles a giant, floating wolf head and can grant wishes. My spies inform me that he once instilled Jake the Filth-Dog with the power of a thousand partying demons. Booya! Bow down, O Reader, to the Party God!

Peppermint Butler I have stated before my innate revulsion toward any humanoid whose flesh is composed of candy. Such a being is

Peppermint Butler, servile minion of Princess Bubblegum. Despite being an insignificant blip upon the Radar-scope of Existence, this sentient breath mint wears many hats in the Candy Kingdom, including valet, chef, and jail custodian. He has also served as my minion during the Nightosphere Celebrity Golf Open. In addition, to his credit, my observant daughter claims he has buried dead bodies on the ninth hole. *Dad, I was kidding. He's just creepy.*

He's one twisted piece of Peppermint!

Hi, baby!

여보!

DUDE, IT'S JUST A PICTURE...

Pig A gangster pig with a stentorian voice who by all reports has been infected by the Scourge of True Love. Even worse to report, this low-life, porcine oaf loves the loathsome being known as Tree Trunks. My daughter claims that the odd couple's uninhibited and open cuddling and kissing has on several occasions induced an epidemic of retching by innocent passersby in the streets of Ooo.

Rainicorns According to the Oooian census, this refers to Ethyl and Bob Rainicorn, two freaks (half horse, half rainbow) and their obnoxious daughter previously described, Lady Rainicorn. The only worthy thing they ever attempted was to devour Finn the Human. Props on that. Otherwise they're typical Oooians whose souls I shall suck as soon as I get my suit back from the cleaners.

Ricardio A favorite among Fans of Ghoulish, Oozing Gore (such as Myself and My Daughter), Ricardio is the humanoid-shaped, disgorged heart of the inexpressibly annoying ninny known as Ice King. When Ricardio escaped from Ice King's scrawny and repulsive chest cavity, he sprouted tiny arms and legs and, with the aid of his new appendages, proceeded to cause havoc and mayhem in the Candy Kingdom. After this unpleasant organ was finally returned to Ice King's body, he vowed to escape again some day. Although he is a veritable imbecile, I endorse his desire to cause chaos and confusion in the smarmy Land of Ooo.

Rump People Fear not, Reader, this interminable List of Insignificants is shortly coming to an end. But until then, behold this race of preening beings with butt-shaped heads who live in the eponymous vale of Rump Town. Due to their unseemly appearance, they tend to despise themselves, and thus I enjoy the company of these creatures more than any other mutant race. A pity they will one day be eaten by my invading demon hordes.

MY MOST HATED PRINCESSES OF OOO
A BRIEF GLOSSARY
BY HUNSON ABADEER, LORD OF EVIL

BREAKFAST PRINCESS
A vomitous Princess composed of a bacon-fat crown, a toast top, pancake skirt, and cracked eggshells for shoes.

COTTON CANDY PRINCESS
A royal humanoid with a grotesque head of pink cotton-candy hair. In her youth, she was kidnapped by the evil Fire Count and saved by the hero Billy. Ho-hum!

This guy's a total loser! Although he IS a delish shade of red...

DR. PRINCESS

A physician at Rock People Hospital who sometimes assists Dr. Ice Cream and Nurse Poundcake.

ELBOW PRINCESS

A blue-green Princess whose head resembles a bent arm, which is how she got her absurd and plebeian moniker.

EMBRYO PRINCESS

This tiny baby Princess can create a protective pink womblike bubble around herself. Eww.

EMERALD PRINCESS

A green-skinned Princess resembling a Russian nesting doll. The only Princess that Ice King has tried to freeze.

ENGAGEMENT RING PRINCESS

This sickeningly cute Candy Kingdom Princess is another semiregular victim of Ice King's Kidnapping Club.

GHOST PRINCESS

The story I got from Marceline: When alive, Ghost Princess was called Warrior Princess and was killed by her lover, Clarence, who later exploded after eating too much cheese. Years later, she forgave Clarence for killing her and they descended to the Nether World together.

HOT DOG PRINCESS

This meaty Ruler of the Hot Dog Kingdom has a crush on Finn and smells like hot dog water.

MUSCLE PRINCESS

A very buff, masculine Princess.
Finn calls her Princess Muscles, and
once tried to steal a lock of her hair.
Tellingly, Ice King considers her the
most beautiful princess of all.

PRINCESS MONSTER WIFE

You call this bag of gore a Princess?
The fact that Ice King stitched
together mutilated Princess parts and
organs to create his own Princess
demonstrates to me, O Demon
Reader, his secret lovable side.

OLD LADY PRINCESS

This elderly Princess was almost
forced to marry Ice King, until Jake
removed her cursed engagement ring
and Ice King married Jake instead.
(Factoid: In the Land of Ooo,
Old Ladies are not humans but a race
of beings who look like Old Ladies.)

PRINCESS PRINCESS PRINCESS

My least favorite Princess
in that she has five heads, and
therefore five mouths with which
to babble and annoy me.

PRINCESS BEAUTIFUL

A mincing skeleton of a Princess
who died of acute baldness.

RAGGEDY PRINCESS

The most delightfully repulsive
Princess in Ooo. She is sometimes
seen flopped in a ditch or a hole,
where I daresay she belongs.

SKELETON PRINCESS

Another undead, fleshless Princess.
Skeleton Princess, also known as
Zombie Princess, rules the Boneyard
Kingdom, likes biting things, and wears
a skirt made of dead bird carcasses.

TOAST PRINCESS

*This thick-sliced member of the
Breakfast royal family rules the
Breakfast Kingdom with her yummy
food-based sister, Breakfast Princess.*

SLIME PRINCESS

*A squat, alligator-kissing Princess
resembling an oozing glob of offal who
rules the underground Slime Kingdom.*

TURTLE PRINCESS

*Head librarian of Ooo and Princess
of the Turtle People. She has a rather
deep voice and is the only Princess
with a second job. One of the many
Princesses who actually wanted
to marry "Nice King," but the
dude rejected her. Psych!*

SPACE ANGEL PRINCESS

*To me, the least likable in Ooo's
Paltry Pantheon of Princesses. Even
her initials spell a veritable sucker.
This winged female from an unknown,
galactic kingdom actually declared
her love for her demented kidnapper.*

WILDBERRY PRINCESS

*This Princess of the Wildberry
Kingdom was rescued twice by the
Oooian dunderheads Finn and Jake.*

Scorcher A silent but deadly hitman of my acquaintance whom Ice King mistakenly hired to assassinate Finn and Jake. Scorcher failed miserably, so I know who not to call if I ever need them destroyed.

Science Know, O Reader, that a humanoid whose flesh is made of candy is a horrific sight to behold. But worse still is a filthy rat made of delicious candy. Half rat, half candy corn, Science is a female of genius intelligence who lives in a cage in Princess Bubblegum's lab. During the Zombie Epidemic, Finn released Science so she would invent a serum to cure the zombies. The sugary rodent succeeded and received a medal for being the first demented, filthy rat to save the Candy Kingdom.

Sharon A sneaky female criminal who became infamous throughout Ooo by disguising herself as the evildoer Gut Grinder. When she was arrested, she confessed that she did it because she wanted to buy things—and picked Jake to frame because he looked hot.

Shelby the Worm
According to my daughter, this is a mincing worm who resides in Jake's viola. In the past I have I advocated force-feeding worms and maggots down the throats of politicians, and Shelby shall be the first when my Politician Worm-Feeding Program begins.

Skeleton Army
My child Marceline's evil army of the undead, which she raised from a graveyard. The Skeleton Army is composed of twelve undead skeletons wielding various deadly weapons and shields. Marceline's magic chant to summon them:

Corpses buried in mud that's black,
From death I command you to come back!

Awkward syntax, but she's young, and anyway, I plan on buying her a deluxe rhyming dictionary.

Pops, I'm over a thousand, remember?

Snail
This seemingly innocuous, insignificant snail is perceived to be everywhere at once in the Land of Ooo. While this might seem an illusion in the minds of video-game addicts, I, Hunson Abadeer, claim that the Snail has been possessed by My Rival in Evil, the second most powerful evil entity in all of the Ooo Universe—The Lich. If true, then the Snail threatens to kill, devour, and thus unexist everyone and everything that exists in the Land of Ooo. Keep your eyes peeled, O Demon Readers, for Slime Trails!

Snorlock
In the infinite variety of entities in an infinite Universe of Evil, the most dreary to focus on is the slug. Yet that is what is being asked of you, O Demon Reader: to focus on the utterly uninteresting slug who mistakenly believes he's a snail. A favor: If I write one more sentence about this humdrum chestnut, I command you to destroy me.

Big talk, Abadeer! We know you're Deathless!

Stag In the annals of esoterica concerning deer, nothing rivals the preposterous Stag who purportedly terrorized all of the Candy Kingdom due to an inexorable desire for candy.

Starchy Although he's not evil, if I were to pick a new best friend, it would be Starchy, a humanoid chocolate malt ball who is also a grave-digger. And if I found I had made a mistake, I could easily have him destroyed once I find someone more compatible.

Susan Strong I have skimmed reports of this Amazon of a currently unknown species living underground with the Hyoomen Tribe—and found them excruciatingly boring. For this reason I suggest you stare at her picture until your visual needs are sated, and then let's begin the Ts.

SHE WAS WEIRD, BUT COOL-WEIRD.

yeah. She let Finn feel under her hat.

SHUT UP, DAWG.

Tree Trunks A pygmy elephant with a southern Ooooian drawl. Normally sweet and naïve, she once bit into a magical apple, transformed into an insane, bloodthirsty overlord of the Crystal Dimension, and tried to turn Finn into her male concubine. Tree Trunks is in a romantic relationship with the porcine ninny known simply as Pig, an unfortunate creature who, when not drenched in barnyard filth, evidently enjoys being cuddled by a love-starved, pygmy elephant.

I'M GONNA GO WITH ABADEER ON THIS ONE.

Undead A category of Ooo inhabitants favored by Yours Truly, which includes Marceline, The Lich, Ghost Princess, Princess Beautiful, Skeleton Princess, Uncle Chewy, and, of course, my old drummer, Death.

Tree Witch Only once in a lifetime is an entity faced with a true terror. And encountering the Human-oid Hag known as Tree Witch means being engulfed in the pit of her *Bottomless Bottom*. I Have Spoken.

THE WHOLE BOTTOMLESS BOTTOM THING GROSSED ME OUT. Dude, I lived it!

Ugly Monster A nettlesome, inconsequential being whose appear-ance here merely serves to fill up the bottom of the page. Shudder briefly and move on, O Demon Reader!

Veggie People A mincing group of plant- and food-based humanoids in Veggie Village, including, inexplicably, sausages and marshmallows. O Demon Reader, is there no end to sausagian and marshmallowic duplicity?

Why-wolves There is nothing more grotesque than a civilized wolf in an Armani suit. The first time a Why-wolf lectured me on Keynesian economics, I had him skinned alive and his epidermis made into a dress for my daughter. *Once again, T.M.I. Dad !!*

Wendy Yet another insignificant prankster who exhibits a common pair of characteristics: a) she is a friend of Marceline; b) she is dead. Will wonders never cease?

Whisper Dan A dark, small-headed, metal creature who served us cheese and crackers when I played poker with Xergiok the Goblin King. I had the distinct impression of barely suppressed insolence; were he not a robot, I suspect he would have secretly spit in our food.

Worm King The leader of a race of worms who invaded the home of Finn and Jake and used his psychic worm powers to make them give him a hug. As for Myself, if I woke up and realized I was the king of a worm colony, I would shove my head into my smoothie blender.

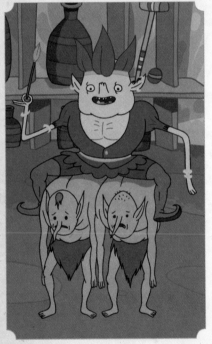

Xergiok Goblin King and one of my poker buddies who still owes me money from a hand of Texas Hold'em. Unfortunately, he is obsessed with spanking his subjects with disturbingly little provocation. Perhaps I've said too much already.

You got that right, Abadeer! HAW!

Zap According to the Annals of Evil, a humanoid in Freak City whom the hobo sorcerer Magic Man transformed into part of the giant known as *Super Freak*. Zap helped Finn and Jake defeat Magic Man, but then decided to remain a part of the Super Freak. As the Hackneyed Saying goes, "Each freak must get his freak on."

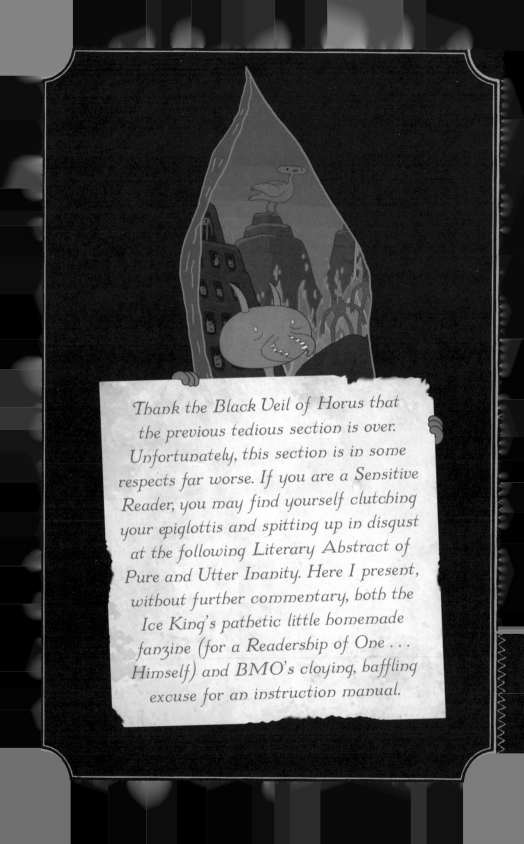

Thank the Black Veil of Horus that the previous tedious section is over. Unfortunately, this section is in some respects far worse. If you are a Sensitive Reader, you may find yourself clutching your epiglottis and spitting up in disgust at the following Literary Abstract of Pure and Utter Inanity. Here I present, without further commentary, both the Ice King's pathetic little homemade fanzine (for a Readership of One . . . Himself) and BMO's cloying, baffling excuse for an instruction manual.

Created by, Conceived by,
Written by, Illustrated by,
and Mimeographed by
The Brainy Bad-boy Behind the
Whole Ice Kingdom Thing...

HIS SUPREME SEXY MAJESTY AND TOTALLY SIIIIIIIIIICK 'ZINE WRITER...

ICE KING!

In this PREMIERE COLLECTOR'S ISSUE NO. 1, we begin with "The Adventures of Fionna and Cake." Enjoy the bios of our characters! Ciao, baby!

Legal Notice: Since this 'zine is bound to make me big money—not only because it's top-quality writing but also because I intend to pass legislation requiring every subject of my kingdom to buy it and read it to the kiddies as a bedtime story every night—and since the characters in "Ooo-La-La!" are definitely in no way based on actual persons inhabiting the Land of Ooo—and since I don't wanna be sued by any inhabitants who think that these characters are in fact based on them and who might try to drag me into some long, drawn-out legal hassle—I'm "mixing it up" so the inhabitants whom my characters are definitely in no way based on won't recognize themselves, and so their lawyers won't have a leg to stand on.

CAKE

Fionna's feline funkster pal and adopted cat sister CAKE is an insufferable, dulcimer-playing furball floozy and a bottomless dispenser of cheap sassitude. Basically a smelly lowlifer, Cake is roughly the size and shape of an overstuffed throw-pillow with legs unless she is, oh, I don't know, ANY OTHER SHAPE AND SIZE SHE WANTS! Because this weird whisker-head has stretchy powers! She can make her legs look like monster mutations made of molasses oozing from her cat torso!!! But so what, I mean, big deal!!! Ice Queen totally does way cooler stuff, right?

Okay, what else about this fuzzy freaky Friday? Oh yeah. Cake got totally hitched to the majestic Lord Monochromicorn (who's way out of her league, by the way, I mean, let's get real!). But it's no secret that, like her sister, Cake would ditch that weirdo in a heartbeat for one lousy date with that paragon of perfection, the Ice Queen!! Seriously, that annoying cat is all about me, I mean, the Ice Queen. But what Fiona and Cake don't realize is that those two are ALWAYS in danger of obliteration at the mighty Ice Queen's perfectly manicured hands, and I'm tellin' ya, folks, it's only a matter of time until the ice pick falls!

FIONNA THE HUMAN GIRL

FIONNA is a feisty little fist-flapping female fool who fancies stuff like swordplay, slush-monster deflection, and Prince-Gumball-butt-saving. Fionna has one weakness—a blinding infatuation with yours truly, Ice King, which transcends the boundaries between her fan-fictional Land of Ooh, in which I don't even exist, and the real Land of Ooo, in which she doesn't exist! Hey, for a figment of my imagination, she's a real cutie. I mean, what a backyard, and what a front yard! (Girls, take note of her white bunny hat, semi-ironic athletic stockings and Mary Janes, all designed to appeal to my, **ahem**, I mean YOUR predilection for postmodern, anime-stylin' fashion culture. Let it not be said that Ice King don't dig Kawaii!!!) But this chick is zilch compared to the incredibly hip ICE QUEEN, into whose frosty embrace Prince Gumball is destined one day to fall, frozen forever in a cryogenic icicle stupor. C'mon, his dopey dalliances with Fionna are obviously just a phase! Just like his flirtations with expressionist gummy sculpture and free-form candy-whistle jazz! But I'll save that Magnificent Wint'ry Wizardess ICE QUEEN till last! See, when I'm excited I get way ahead of myself!

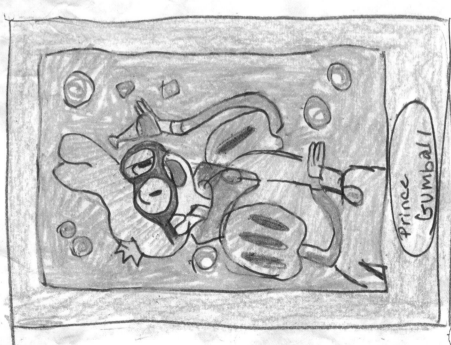

MARSHALL LEE

Marshall is a teen vampire king with a tendency to be awesome with a capital A. This emo, gothy guy likes to chow down on the color red. Maybe because I made him up and he doesn't really exist, sometimes he can be a little sulky, but deep down he seems to be a decent kid. He wears trendy gothy duds like there"s no tomorrow, has a primo electric guitar, doesn't take any baloney from anybody, and has the collective angst of being eighteen for, like, a million years in a row. Even though he's a super-independent homie, Marshall Lee still bows down and gives major props to the hippest super-chill chick who rules over the frozen tundra, the one and only Ice Queen! Not exactly a hipster, but I bet he wouldn't throw away a vintage vest, skinny jeans, Buddy Holly glasses, and a knitted cap if I stuffed 'em in his flutophone case. This kid's mellow yellow and generally a happy camper, but he's not exactly a people-pleaser by a long-shot. Hey, you want some advice, Marshy? If you wanna win over Fionna the Human like I think you do, then what better way than loosening her up with some Truth or Dare and then serenading her with cool rock ballads all about Ice King's exploits?!

PRINCE GUMBALL

The young ruler of the Candy Kingdom is the unfathomably lucky and undeserving object of the Ice Queen's affections. Despite being a mincing moron, Prince Gumball shall one day take his place as the Ice Queen's coruler (in name only) of the Ice Kingdom and as her brainless, groveling love slave. As previously mentioned, Gumball is temporarily distracted from appreciating the Ice Queen's perfectly chiseled features because he likes Fionna the Human, whose fabulous outfits, to be designed by me, probably have him fooled into thinking she's Got It Going On—when instead she fails miserably to know even what It Is and most assuredly Does Not Have It Going On Nowhere Nohow!

Prince Gumball is notable for an inability to defend himself from being blasted against his own bedroom wall by the Ice Queen's awesome Slush Monster or encased in a giant icicle hanging from the ceiling. He also is known to have designed his own royal garb and to enjoy baking. I'll come up with some more good stuff later. That's just for starters!

THE ICE QUEEN

Yes! We've come to the best part, baby! Winter's
wrath incarnate! Absolute zero on wheels! Goddess of
howling winds and lip-chapping, flesh-searing cold!
White-haired and dazzling in her icy blue finery, she
breaks hearts and crushes souls wherever she blows!
What a dame! Far more intelligent and powerful than
any other being in the fan-fictional Land of Ooh, the
lonely Ice Queen longs for a companion worthy of her
magnificence. Tragically, the closest thing she can
find is that buffoon Prince Gumball, while the only
being who could ever truly sweep the Ice Queen off
her frostbitten feet is, well, me, Ice King! But
that's not gonna happen, because I exist in the real
reality, whatever that is! Oh, my Ice Queen, my fan-
fiction figment of fabulosity, one day I shall
freeze and shatter all time and space, pulverizing
the very confines of existence into harmless snow-
flakes, which'll float dreamily around us as we gaze
into each other's beady black eyes, together forever
at last!

LORD MONOCHROMICORN

This classy, sky-high playa plays loyal steed and
best friend to Prince Gumball but is actually way
cooler than the Prince because he can do stuff like
hide inside a cloud, snap his tail like a whip, roll
himself into a giant spiral, and speak Morse! I mean,
he speaks in Morse code only! How cool is that?? Like
Prince Gumball, Monochromicorn shows exceptionally poor
taste in females since he ended up with Cake, the
skuzzy chubby kitty who has a bad attitude and can't
even fly. I mean, what's that about? Lord Monochromicorn
is jet black and cold gray and trails awesome
thunderbolts through the sky wherever he goes. How
great is that?
  This serpentine dude will make a fearsome addition to
  the Ice Queen's court, color-complementing some of
  her cool outfits and striking terror in the hearts of
  his former Candy Kingdom compatriots who used to ask
  him for his autograph constantly because he lied to
  Cake about playing in a ska band with me a long time
  ago and she told everyone.

INSTRUCTIONAL PAMPHLET AND USER'S GUIDE

CONGRATULATIONS!

You are now the proud owner of a cutting-edge, handheld, mash-up, multi-user gaming device with individual simultaneous computron controllers and Vectrex reverse-prefix modulators.

이것은 제조업체가 BMO 장치의 부적절하거나 적절한 사용으로 인한 위험에 대한 책임을지지 의미하지 않는다.

플립 모듈을 조정

악어 클립 조여
36

05

31

거꾸로하다

14

올려 스핀을 들어

Zip! Whir! Buzz! We know you'll
enjoy with your new factory-fresh
mobile friend-simulator...

BMO!

28

코드 설정

42

1. **Adjust Flip Module**
2. **Set Code with Flange Key**
3. **Reverse Fun Activator**
4. **Test Voltage Slot Chip**
5. **Degauss Sunshine Strip**
6. **Lift & Spin Smile Grip**
7. **Install & Lock Pinky Pin**
8. **Connect Bunny Ground**
9. **Push-Pull Aztec Crimper**
10. **Enjoy Reverse Polarity Fun!**

17

핀 활성화

2

87

설치 및 잠금

이것은 제조업체가 BMO
장치의 부적절하거나 적절한
사용으로 인한 위험에 대한
책임을지지 의미하지 않는다.

푸시 - 당겨지지는 사람

Remember one thing~BMO is sweet!

Even when not being played, BMO's durable and attractive, 8-bit, optimized, real-time supranet face-plate design with its trademarked name, "BMO," printed on the side is a winner in any geekster's Fortran redux server interface. Moreover, BMO has a handy convertible input slot for VHS or Beta tapes, and a button under its zaftig ream controller's D-pad will send a digital target signal directly into its Main Brain Game Frame. BMO's various mono and stereo attachments facilitate E-Z operation of 16-track simul-editing software for basic audio packet recording protocols, as well as network with virtually any linear filmmaking software plug-ins, recharge other devices, and allow instant correction for alarm clock settings and camera functions for recording maximum Adorable Cuteness Imagery (ACI) when confronted by rainbows, puppies, or unicorns!

BMO's Talky Fun Sound!

Whose voice has fuzzy enjoyment? Well, it is true! Acoustic experiments of science confirm BMO vox makes Top Magic Fun Time! BMO Vibratory Menu has notable and adorable cuteness like candy for Ear Holes! Hear the enjoyment during sunshine or the night-time! Such many noises…for YOU!

위험이은 금지합니다!

BMO's charming voice simulation default, "Adorable Child," was tested on a focus group of twenty hideous Nightsphere demons locked in steel cages by our test-wizards. After hearing BMO's incredibly cute voice simulation, they were released and monitored, and in each case went out and bought puppies and kittens.

III

THE LAND OF OOO AND YOU

TO BE READ *in the* DEEPEST TONES *of* SARCASM

As Lord of Evil of the Nightosphere, my Goal is twofold: First, to suck the souls from every Creature in Ooo (save that of my daughter Marceline, of course). And second, to Obliterate the existence of the Land of Ooo and thus render the Universe free of all Ooooian Influence.

Book III shall give you, the Demon Reader, precise directions to this evil goal. But if you'd rather skip this and flip ahead to the grittier chapters, I shall sum things up:

1. First, shudder in fear in the presence of these, My Evil Words.

2. After exhibiting the proper amounts of fear and trembling, get your passport stamped at the Nightosphere Customs Office and then enter the Despised Land of Ooo.

3. Once there, begin annoying Oooian Inhabitants. Suggestions: Play out-of-tune, electric lutes at high volume, substitute regular drinking glasses with Joke Dribble Glasses, place Whoopie Cushions on every royal throne in this Detestable Realm, and so on. Catch my drift, O Abominable Demons? I have spoken.

Although I had initially planned to insert
Nightosphere Warfare Maps here—
showing the military weaknesses of the
Kingdoms of Ooo—to encourage other lands
to attack, cause mayhem, and destroy,
I found some cute travel stuff
I thought I'd use instead. Let us begin
with the following unbearably jejune
(and vile in its unrelenting sweetness)
travel brochure created by Princess
Bubblegum to encourage tourism in her
Kingdom of Repugnant Confections and
throughout the Despised Environs of Ooo...

Princess Bubblegum's

Here's a little travel brochure to give visitors some tips on where to find primo candy and scientific anomalies in each Kingdom!

OFFICIAL
TRAVEL
GUIDE
to the
CANDY KINGDOM
and Beyond!

The CANDY KINGDOM!

One of the most popular destinations, at the heart of my kingdom, would have to be my scrumptious castle. Nestled in a valley of the pinkest cotton candy, surrounded by lollipops and built upon the finest peanut brittle, it is made entirely of sugary sweets. Our moat and drawbridge (actually a huge piece of toast with jam) are watched over 24/7 by the Guardians of the Royal Promise. Be sure to get a picture of that!

Make your way to the vanilla-ice-cream-flavored Central Tower. From there you can visit the Grand Hall, large enough to hold all of my candy subjects without any getting stuck together. You might meet Chocoberry, Mr. Cupcake, Chet, Starchy, Cinnamon Bun, or the Marshmallow Kids! In case of medical emergencies, see Nurse Poundcake or Dr. Ice Cream. Peppermint Butler is at your service as concierge, and for the adventurous... the Ice Cream Bar!

Like most cities, The Candy Kingdom has a seedier side. The Candy Tavern is a popular little roadhouse in the back alley behind my castle. Jaybird and his gang hang out there, too, so enter at your own risk and hide your valuables!

Remember: Everything is edible, but you can't eat anything that talks! As my friend Finn the Human says, "They got aspirations."

The FIRE KINGDOM!

The Fire Kingdom is one of the hottest vacation spots in the Great Northwest. It is home to most of the Fire Elementals of Ooo. One of my favorite inhabitants is Flambo, who just loves to help me throw my royal barbecues. He sets a few random fires here and there, but he has a warm heart. In fact, if you're uncomfortable with the heat, have Flambo cast a spell on you so you don't burn or melt to death!

One of the scientific anomalies here is that the inhabitants die if it rains. Frown face! Tip: Bring a fire-retardant umbrella. In a rainstorm, save a Fire Creature and get free Tourist Swag!

I recommend a lovely picnic area on the border of the Grass Lands and the Fire Kingdom. But keep your eyes peeled for the Fire Wolves! They can burst into flame for no apparent reason—a problem if you forgot your fire-retardant outerwear!

This kingdom of hotties is made up mostly of volcanoes overlooking great seas of molten lava. Be sure to set your fashion dial to light and summery!

Flame King currently rules the Fire Kingdom. He has a very hip teenage daughter, but you need to catch her on a good day.

The ICE KINGDOM!

Need to cool off? Try the Wintry Wonderland known as the Ice Kingdom! This frozen waste-land—I mean, Vacation Paradise—is home to glaciers, snowy peaks, and fragrant penguins. Oh, and don't forget those golem ice creatures and the Iceclops!

No need to decide which lovely resort to book in this snow-man's paradise, because Ice King's Castle is the ONLY place to stay! The castle is actually a hollow, pointy, snowcapped mountain surrounded by nothing but that white winter stuff! It all overlooks the aptly named Iceberg Lake. See if you can spot the frozen businessmen dotting the shore!

When visiting the Ice Castle, keep an eye out for the cage where that incorrigible old Ice King keeps captive princesses. He's got secret chambers galore, assorted ice monsters, and a basement filled with the latest in technology and fine ninja memorabilia!

Looking for the perfect place for your nuptials? According to the Ice King, a traditional Ice Kingdom wedding involves binding up the bride, lowering her on a rope, and touching her to the groom's beard! The ropes allegedly bring good luck to the marriage!

LUMPY SPACE!

You'll marvel at Lumpy Space's lovely elm trees and lumpy clouds in shades of purple and blue! But if your teens drag you to someplace oranger and greener, beware! This is Makeout Point, where bad kids do strange things to make themselves look "smoother" (and, of course, "make out"). Instead, why not take the kids to Lumpy Space School, where Lumpy Space Princess had her Fifteenth Birthday Bash?!

Lumpy Space itself is a cloudlike cityscape in deep space and is home to the teen-friendly Lumpy Space People! The locals are an interesting group and have their own unique culture, as will be apparent pretty quickly. They tend to have a negative view of "non-lumpers" or "smoothies," as outsiders are called. If you find yourself at Lumpy Space Saloon, watch out, the partying can be intense!

To get to Lumpy Space, head for the Cotton Candy Forest on the border of the Desert of Doom. The portal is cleverly disguised as a frog sitting on a mushroom. The password is "Whatevers2009," but your teens might have to say it, just to get the right inflection!

The BREAKFAST KINGDOM!

If you're pressed for time, why not try the Breakfast Kingdom? Ruled by Breakfast Princess and Toast Princess, it would make a lovely weekend getaway for those in need of a quick bite. This petite, beautifully designed kingdom sits at the end of Brunch Canyon. The castle itself is a giant coffee percolator situated atop a giant dish of coffee cake and fried eggs! Fresh oranges grow in the courtyard for your fresh-squeezing pleasure, and the castle is surrounded by a moat of steaming hot coffee, accessed by several crispy bacon bridges.

If you're on a limited budget, consider the Hot Dog Kingdom, which is more of a micro-nation than an actual kingdom. It is quite modest, really, as it's just a simple wooden gate around a small yard, with a small doghouse attached. I suppose that's why this is a less costly destination. You get what you pay for, right, fellow travelers?

The HOT DOG KINGDOM!

Controlled by the Hot Dog Princess and well guarded by her Hot Dog Knights, the Hot Dog Kingdom is still prone to mischief! I read a recent report about several Battle Cubes attacking Hot Dog Princess from the sky.

...and two more WILD locations!

Those with a brave heart might want to take a trip to the Spooky Forest. Just south of the Haunted Swamp in the Land of Ooo, this freaky forest is known for its gnarled dead trees and its dark pathways to nowhere. When walking alone at night, notice that the trees have gaping, mouthlike openings. No worries— I'm sure it's nothing.

In this neighborhood, you'll also come upon the infamous ghost mansion at 25 Blood Drive, the premier party pad for many local vampires and spooks. Ask for Wendy, Booboo, or Georgy if you want an invite, but keep your eyes open wide.

Well, that's about it! Don't forget to bring a compass, sextant, and fire extinguisher in case you're lost in the grungier areas or eaten by Fire Wolves. Most important of all, if you meet me, don't eat me! Eating Princesses is punishable by Life Imprisonment with No Sweets for Life! Got it?

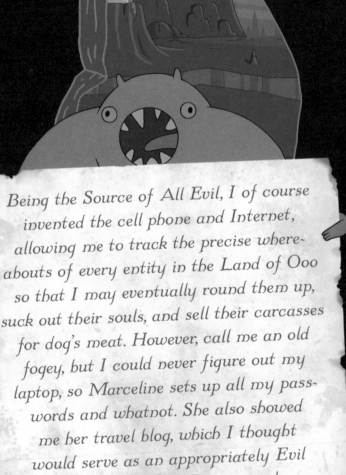

Being the Source of All Evil, I of course invented the cell phone and Internet, allowing me to track the precise whereabouts of every entity in the Land of Ooo so that I may eventually round them up, suck out their souls, and sell their carcasses for dog's meat. However, call me an old fogey, but I could never figure out my laptop, so Marceline sets up all my passwords and whatnot. She also showed me her travel blog, which I thought would serve as an appropriately Evil Chapter Ending. Bon voyage!

MARCELINE'S

TRAVEL BLOG FOR DEMON BACKPACKERS

BENEATHAVERSE

If you like dark, rocky underground kingdoms (and who doesn't?) then you will enjoy a trip down a secret portal and into the land of Beneathaverse. It is a well-hidden, cramped domain run by Gnome Ruler and his mini Gnome Minions. This location is so top secret that I never even knew about it until my friend Finn was kidnapped, right outside of his Tree Fort, and forced down the well. I'll admit, his stay there was not very relaxing, as the Gnome Ruler hooked him up to various machines to try to harness his power. But that was a bit of an overreach, and I think they may have backed off. Anyway, I love it down beneath there because it is very dark, dank, and the entire city is built within a large underground cavern. Makes me feel right at home.

THE OOO CEMETERY

One of my other favorite haunts is the Hamburger Hills Cemetery. Nobody ever notices me there, because it is the kind of place you can go to be alone. It is mainly Ghosts and a few Spirit Waves hanging out. Not many undead creatures. All the old gravestones are transparent and are bright neon orange. I love to go there and sit on a picnic blanket and write lyrics. It is so relaxing and quiet. It appears to have been established long before the Mushroom War even, since it has ruins and other modern-day objects scattered around. There are winding cement stairs and decaying mausoleums. It is well worth a day trip for a nice restful place to chillax.

GOBLIN KINGDOM

If you love beautiful architecture, you must go visit the Goblin Kingdom. The Throne Room, the Dragon Stables, and the Garden of the Living Fountains are all exquisite. Too bad the local Goblins have to stink the whole place up, though. Sorry, not trying to be rude. I heard that Gummy, the Royal Chief of Staff, was actually a pretty good guy. But as a general rule, Goblins and I don't mix that well. I know that King Xergiok was kind of a jerk, and he liked to spank his subjects, which is weird, but I really love his taste in palatial structures. Be sure to save some time to visit the Royal Game Archive too. The Goblin Birthing Pits I could do without, though.

THE GRASS LANDS

The Grass Lands are my old stomping grounds. They're kind of like the suburbs of Ooo, as it seems nearly everyone I know lives there. Finn and Jake live in my old Tree House, and also BMO, Tree Trunks, Neptr, Hot Dog Princess, Science Cat, Shark, Fuzzy Friends, the Two-headed Duck, Donny and the House People, Jiggler and his Mama, Banana Man, the Tree Witch, Shelby, Snail, Worm, Snake, the Battle Cubes . . . you get the idea. Everybody seems to live in and around these green, centrally located fields.

Back in the day, this area was called the Verdant Plains. It shares borders with the Candy Kingdom, the Ice Kingdom, and the Fire Kingdom, so it is kind of the heart of Ooo. I moved away and found a nice cave so I could get away from all this normalcy. Sometimes the rainbows, blue skies, and green fields are too much for me.

BEAUTOPIA

Located deep within a cave system that Finn and Jake discovered under a hatch lies what was once a luxury coastal resort, now collapsed in ruins. After the Lub Glubs drove the Hyoomens out, they were forced to retreat to the garbage heaps near the entrance hatch. It looks like an old abandoned mall, as multiple storefronts can still be seen. At the center of Beautopia, there is a tower-like structure, which acts as underground lighting source for the whole city. Once the fires are stoked and the main tower is lit up, all the other little fires light up as well. It is actually quite beautiful, hence the name, I guess. This is a good place to hibernate and to escape the flowers and rainbows for a while.

LAND OF THE DEAD

OK, this is like another dimension where all the disparate souls go and mingle after their mortals croak. It's mostly inhabited by skeletons hoping to find some flesh to eat, various bloodsucking insects, and assorted creatures of the underworld. The place is littered with bones, old tires, crashed flying saucers, and wrecked patrol cars … it's awesome.

You have to get past the Gate Guardian, who patrols the main escalator, which only moves one way, and that is DOWN. Nobody expects anyone to be coming back up in the other direction. But once you get past that knucklehead, a lot of cool things lie ahead.

The main attraction is Death's Castle. Constructed entirely of light, it's eerie, glowing, transparent, and it's the only light in the entire land. Yeah, Death is a bit of a drama queen, but this is his world, and it *does* revolve around him.

THE NIGHTOSPHERE

The Nightosphere is an alternate dimension inhabited by my annoying Dad, Hunson Abadeer, and a multitude of other demonic and "deathless" entities. The secret portal between it and Ooo was formed in my house. OK, so it does happen to be a demonic wasteland filled with utter chaos and an array of dysfunctional

I'm not saying this place is for everybody. It does have its problems. It's entirely engulfed in flames, for one thing. It's way overcrowded, and on top of that, I think my father is considering charging an entry fee at some point. But in case anyone wants to have a look-see, here are the instructions.

HOW TO GET THERE:

1. First draw the PHIL FACE (happy face).
2. Then douse it with Bug Milk.
3. Then chant, in Latin, "*Maloso vobiscum et cum spiritum!*"
4. Boom. You're there.

SWAMP OF EMBARRASSMENT

All right, I only included this place because it is the best place I know of to prank people. Just take anyone there, and it is sure to be a horrendously awkward situation. Check it out. It's packed full of naked old people, and they are not too shy to make a scene.

They are always buck naked, and older than dirt, and taking showers behind these big reddish curtains. They get angry and call people "perverts" if they have to walk past. Or sometimes they yell loudly, "My most private parts!" as you are trying to get through. My friend Finn had to go through the swamp, while his face turned beet red, on his quest to get the Armor of Zeldron. That still cracks me up thinking about it, because he's so shy. So if you have anyone you want to embarrass, this swamp is the perfect destination.

These are just a few highlights of my recent travels. I can't really go into too many details, because I do cherish my wicked privacy. I'll add that 50th Dead World is a cool place to hang out, too, but if you wanted to join me, I'm afraid I would have to kill you first.

Hey, Marceline, that was cool. Way better than your Dad's stuff!

Thanks, Jake. :)

IV

THE LOST TEXTS OF OOO

IN WHICH
the UNSPEAKABLE is SPOKEN

In this, Book IV, the most controversial book of this Magnificent Encyclopaedia for the Edification of Demons, Heroes, and Wizards, all cosmic bets are off, and many time-worn secrets are at last revealed and laid waste. In this, the opening section, I present the legendary Lost Texts of Ooo. Only recently were these ancient scrolls unearthed, in a manner that will make the Demon Reader's day and turn the Hero Reader's stomach with queasiness and disgust.

Ironically, most of the Ancient Secrets in these texts will appear incredibly dull and boring to uninitiated, insouciant, or naïve readers who perhaps have long gray beards, a wise countenance, and impressive credentials, but who are in fact self-absorbed imbeciles devoid of inward-turned, cosmic eyes with which to perceive The Truth of That Which Is.

Book IV of the Encyclopaedia of Ooo contains Ineffable Fragments from Ancient Texts, as well as a catalogue of Arcane Spells and Secrets that were erased from Reality by Mind Police Wizards, only recently recovered and restored to their full glory in this present Unparalleled Literary Magnum of Intoxicating Magnficence.

With this serried admission, and warning of encroaching nausea, let the Lost Book Four of the Encyclopaedia of Ooo now begin.

THE ENCHIRIDION: BOOK OF HEROES

GAUCHE EXCERPTS
SELECTED *by the* CURATOR
at the
HADES ARCHIVES
of the NIGHTOSPHERE MUNICIPAL LIBRARY

*T*he *Enchiridion* is an ancient book originally guarded by Mannish Man the Minotaur and later in the possession of Finn the Human. This book is known throughout Ooo as being the Final Word on All Things Heroic. It has also been proven effective to use to hit someone on the back who is choking, perhaps on a stubborn piece of steak.

The Enchiridion's History, Origin, and Authorship are unknown. However, the ancient photograph opposite shows Simon Petrikov *before* the Mushroom War with what may or may not be the original copy of Ooo's legendary *Book of Heroes*.

The Enchiridion is coded with secrets of supreme importance, and were it to fall into the hands of The Lich, or any Creature Possessed by The Lich, the inevitable decline of Physical Reality would result.

Unless, of course, it doesn't. You never know these days. But the book's involuntary ensconcement by forces of evil certainly won't be anything to jump up and down about.

CHAPTER FOUR
DIDACTIC PADDING
That The Hero Should Duly Ignore

BRAVE HERO, LET YOUR SWORD BE SHEATHED, FOR THOUGH IT BE YOUR BEST AND MOST TRUSTY TOOL, IT CANNOT HELP YOU WHEN TRAVERSING THE TREACHEROUS TERRAIN UPON WHICH YOU NOW EMBARK. A GREAT WARRIOR MUST SCALE THE HIGHEST TOWERS, MAIM THE WICKED, AND THROTTLE AGILE DEMONS, BUT THESE CHALLENGES

CHAPTER FIVE
HOW TO KISS A PRINCESS

KISSING A PRINCESS IS DIFFERENT THAN KISSING YOUR GRANDMOTHER OR YOUR MOTHER. VERY DIFFERENT. A PECK ON THE CHEEK IS NOT GOING TO CUT IT. NOTHING BUT LIP-ON-LIP ACTION WILL SUFFICE WITH A TRUE PRINCESS. IT'S BEST TO FIRST PRACTICE ON A LIP MONSTER, BUT PROCEED

WITH CAUTION BECAUSE, AS EVERYONE KNOWS, A LIP MONSTER CAN EASILY KISS THE UNTRAINED HERO TO DEATH!

CHAPTER TEN
THE CYCLOPS

DEEP IN THE FOREST OF TREES, THERE IS A CYCLOPS WHOSE MAGICAL TEARS CAN HEAL ANY WOUND. SKIP THIS SENTENCE, SO THAT THE WARRIOR CAN BEGIN THE NEXT SENTENCE, THE REALLY GOOD ONE. WHAT CYCLOPSES LACK IN DEPTH PERCEPTION, THEY MAKE UP FOR IN BEING REALLY TALL AND CRYING A LOT. THEY HAVE PRETTY BAD EMOTIONAL

CHAPTER FOURTEEN
AVOIDING PITFALLS AND TRAPS

NOT ALL MORTAL DANGER ARRIVES IN THE GUISE OF UNDEAD WARRIORS OR TOWERING MONSTERS! A TRUE HERO MASTERS THE WATCHFUL ARTS, RECOGNIZES THE SCENT OF DANGER BEFORE IT APPEARS, AND UNDERSTANDS CARELESSNESS IS THE FIANCÉE OF DOOM!

HAIL THE BRAVE SHIRKER WHO SOARS AWAY UNSCATHED ON WINGS OF AVOIDANCE!

A TRAP MAY TAKE A THOUSAND FORMS, FROM AN UNLIT FIRECRACKER CLEVERLY WEDGED IN DOG MUCK TO A BOOBYTRAPPED MINESHAFT THAT ENTOMBS THE LUCKLESS ADVENTURER WITHIN ITS CAVERNOUS DEPTHS

What time is it? DOODLETIME!!!

SPELLS AND SECRETS
OF THE
LAND OF OOO

기여우 기여우

Oooian Anthropologists found the dangerous texts of Book Three, which had been hidden by Ancient Mind Police Wizards, etched on iron plates in the skulls of desiccated demon warriors in the Lava Sea of the Nightosphere.

It seems that early Nightospherean demons and gargoyles were brain fetishists and trepanned themselves as a sign of eminence. The greatest demon warriors and chiefs had customized trepanning done: They had engraved iron plates slid into slots in their heads, and on those plates were chiseled mysterious texts of vulgate demonic writing. The following priceless texts of the Lost Legends of Ooo were translated from plates recovered out of the heads of thirty-nine ancient demon warriors in a sacred burial ground excavated beneath My Summer Palace in East Nightosphere, north of the Va-Va-Voom Dance Vomitorium and southwest of Chester's Human Flesh Hot Dog Stand.

The plates were removed from the charred, horned skulls of these unearthed demon warriors with meat tongs in a manner too inefficacious and unpleasant to explicate to any children who may be reading. However, since I now cast a spell upon This page forcing all children to fall into a dull stupor, I shall now explain every grotesque surgical procedure in minute, disgusting detail.

step 1: Wash and scrub claws free of any vermin entrails residue with distilled Hydrofluoric Acid (being careful to refrain from drinking it, despite its delicious, acrid flavor, zesty afterburn. Allow the acid to thorough~ ~can-

and so we begin the first of the following precious and monumental Lost Texts of Ooo transcribed from metal plates surgically removed from the skulls of demons, beginning with Legend the First, the most important text in all of history, which reveals the secret meaning behind sentient existence itself, and why there is something instead of Nothing.

~ ~ ~not eat the whole egg to !

LEGEND THE FIRST

he secret Reason for and Means by which the Fecund Pundament of the Universe created and uncreated itself out of nothing is absurdly simple, and can be explained in one sentence containing no big words, a sentence so clear and concise that even a senile, butt-scratching cave goblin can understand it, and that sentence is "There is a difference betw

HEYYY, WHAT HAPPENED TO THE SECRET OF THE UNIVERSE ???

What a rip-off!

~o, aside from revealing the secret meaning and origin of the self-created universe, the preceding legends also explain why women's noses do not emit snores as loudly as those of men, and how much money the Entire Universe is worth in gold Oooian centurians, and who can afford it, and why on some days you awaken with a perfectly coiffed hair skull-covering, and on other days you awaken to find your hair resembling the Nest of a headless Neck-oozing reptile from the swamp of the Many and the infamous stenches.

ABADEER INDUSTRIES NOVELTY SPELLS and CURSES

OVERNIGHT DELIVERY AVAILABLE
...TIED TO THE OLAWS OF A SHRIEKING KRAKEN

.........AI898

SEVERED CLAW—A new twist on a tired old prank! Instead of a gag, this spell actually severs a victim's claw! Imagine the sound of your sucker's shrieks!...................AI5543

PARTY BLOOD GULP—Banish boredom with a spell to transform any punch bowl into a cauldron of coagulated gore! Great for birthdays, proms, graduations!.................AI119

CATFLAPS—Mewling pests infesting your cozy cave? Slap a cat-sized portal on any wall or door, or toss one on the floor for an instant, bottomless bye-bye hole!...........AI3449

REPLACE PEANUTS—Replace a party peanut bowl with entirely different peanuts! Imagine their face as they chomp on new, unfamiliar peanuts! Fun! Idiotic!.................AI491

INVENT DANCE MOVE—The dance floor can be a prison...a prison for sheep! Now you can conjure your own signature dance move and break with the herd! AI7411

DIVIDE BY SEVEN—Pop quiz: How many times does seven go into 70? It's a mathemagical mystery! Know for sure with this amazing spell for evil imbeciles!...................AI421

NOMENCLATURUS—PERMANENTLY RENAME annoyingly titled creatures! Humiliate the pretentious with new names like Chumpy, Seamus O'Grambo, or even Amelia DuBois!........A2382

RING O' BEEF—One dash of magic seasoning salt and a bloody hoop of cow intestine encircles and entangles your target! Especially upsetting to vegetarians!............AI2321

CHARLEY COW—This little known cousin of the charley horse delivers the same intense cramping but with the mortifying bonus of nonstop milk production!..............AI2235

MEDIOCRITIZE—A welcome boost for the lazy, and a remedy for the ambitious! Forces any demon into the "Goldilocks Zone"—not too good, not too bad!. AI809

HAMSTERIZE—Grants any demon a pair of infinitely extensible cheeks! Ideal for armless adventurers or handless housewives in need of storage space........................AI249

SLEEVE TALLY—What were your sleeves like yesterday? Last week? Last year? Cast this spell and watch your arm's fashion history flash before your bloodshot eyes!.........AI445

ELDERSCENT—Imbues any demon with a delicate, grandmotherly odor. With hints of lavender, rosewater, ancient peppermint, and intestinal parasites. AI1175

No offense, Pops, but you _know_ most of these spells are bogus. They only work if you're a dork.

HUNSON ABADEER'S
DEALS TO DIE FOR!

HELLO, WANNABE WIZARDS! LORD OF EVIL HERE! I'VE HAND-PICKED THE WORST OF THE WORST MAGICAL SPELLS AND CURSES, GUARANTEED TO GIVE YOU BELLY LAUGHS AT YOUR VICTIM'S BLOOD-CURDLING SHRIEKS! **ALL** AT ROCK-BOTTOM PRICES! **NEW! NOVEL! SENSATIONAL! GORY!** STUPID HOLLOW DIVERSIONS TO SIMULATE MEANING IN EVEN THE MOST POINTLESS DEMONIC EXISTENCE!

LEGAL DISCLAIMER: THESE SPELLS, TRANSLATED FROM THE BRAIN PLATES OF ANCIENT DEMON CON MEN, MAY OR MAY NOT WORK AS INDICATED, OR MAY SIMPLY KILL YOU. ENJOY!

NECROMANCY— Famously used by The Lich and Marceline, this spell brings dead bodies to life as the wizard's obedient slaves! Fresh corpses? No problem! Skeletal remains? Child's play! NOTHING is too dead for this spell! Results guaranteed!................HB24

GENERATE MAYONNAISE— Finally, a spell to create mayonnaise at will! Great for demons who love mayo and scorpion hoagies...HB22

BLAZING FEET—Confuse your enemy! Set your feet on fire without any pain! Or WITH pain, if you prefer! It's up to YOU!...................HB0414

MAGICUS NOMOREICUSS— A very useful spell that strips another wizard of all magical abilities! Turns an all-powerful wizard into a helpless baby!..........HB2388

SHADOWCERY—Creates Shadow Golems imbued with consciousness. As every demon knows, Shadows have a delightfully dark aftertaste. Bon appétit!............HB055

MACRONANCY—Changes any wizard into a 50-foot giantess named Nancy Lynne Kitchins. Tower over enemies! Impress friends with bigger excretions!.................HB1029

DUSTOMANCY—Simply eat a broom and gain magical control of dust motes! Hours of entertainment for nearsighted demon dimwits!.......HB12118

VORPAL HAND—Demonic warrior's spell that transforms your hand into a deadly sword. Cuts anything! Never be caught "unarmed" again!............HB292

HAIR GROWTH—Balding demons adapted this spell to shave a century off their appearance. Enjoy supple new claws and gleaming, luxurious scales!.........HB115

DRAGON EYES—Gives a wizard the eyes of a dragon. Trade them for various nerd collectables at the Nightosphere's Demon Gorecon!...................HB1225

GO BACKICUS FROM WHENCE YOU CAMEICUS— This spell, popular among witches, banishes anyone back to the place they came from...........................HB334

KEE OTH RAMA PANCAKE —A wonderfully effective spell for demons or Oooie dogs to banish unwant- ed enemies or tiresom friends.......................HB559

V

FORBIDDEN CHAPTERS
IN THE ENCYCLOPÆDIA
OF 000

UNLIKE ERUDITE ENCYCLOPAEDIAS WRITTEN BY SCHOLARLY FOOLS,
THE BOOK YOU NOW HOLD IN YOUR CLAWS IS DIFFERENT
IN A FUNDAMENTAL WAY:

I KNOW IT'S KINDA COOL, BUT I'VE GOT NO IDEA WHAT THESE WORDS MEAN.

IT IS ALIVE.

Um, cuz you're a Numbskull? Actually... me neither.

I, HUNSON ABADEER, HAVE CONJURED IT TO BE SO,
HAVING INSTILLED IN EVERY PAGE AND IN EVERY WORD AND IN EVERY
ILLUSTRATION THE ABILITY TO TRANSMOGRIFY AT WILL ACCORDING TO
THE WHIM OR DESIRE OF THE BOOK ITSELF. THUS EACH TIME IT IS READ,
THE WORDS, ILLUSTRATIONS, AND DECORATIVE FESTOONMENTS MAY BE
THE SAME, MAY BE SOMEWHAT DIFFERENT, OR MAY CHANGE
TO CREATE A NEW BOOK ENTIRELY.

FOR THIS REASON, WHEN THE FIRST PRINTING OF THIS BOOK WAS DISTRIBUTED
TO BOOKSTORES IN THE NIGHTOSPHERE METROPOLIS, MANY DEMONS WHO
READ IT WENT COMPLETELY AND UTTERLY MAD. LAWSUITS EVENTUATED DUE
TO THE FACT THAT THE NIGHTOSPHERE IS INHABITED MAINLY BY ATTORNEYS,
AS WELL AS THEIR RESEARCHERS, SECRETARIES, AND ASSISTANTS. TO AVOID
FURTHER LITIGATION, DEMON EDITORS OF SUBSEQUENT EDITIONS
REMOVED THE CHAPTERS MOST IMBUED WITH THE MAGICAL
UMBRA OF TRANSMOGRIFICATION. *???*

IN THOSE MAGICALLY DRAINED EDITIONS, THE RESIDUE OF MAGIC MADE
THE TEXT MORE OR LESS THE SAME AT EVERY READING WITH SLIGHT CHANGES
THAT WERE BARELY PERCEPTIBLE: AN ILLUSTRATION WOULD BE REVERSED, A WORD
CHANGED TO ITS SYNONYM, ETC. IN THIS COMMEMORATIVE EDITION, HOWEVER,
I HAVE DEPURGATED THE AMBIGUITY FROM MISSING CHAPTERS AND RESTORED
THEM TO THEIR FORMER GLORY, READY TO DRIVE READERS MAD.

HERE, THEN, AT THE END OF THE BOOK, ARE THE MOST DANGEROUS
IF NOT OUTRIGHT DEADLY CHAPTERS OF THE ENCYCLOPAEDIA OF OOO,
BOUND TOGETHER WITH THIS WARNING, THE TEXT ITSELF ABLE TO TRICK
AND MANIPULATE THE READER IN VARIEGATED PERMUTATIONS OF DECEIT
AND SIMULACRA OF FALSITY. ?!!

ONLY THE MOST BOLD OR FORMIDABLE READERS
SHOULD READ PAST THIS POINT. IF YOU ARE NOT INCREDIBLY STRONG,
I SUGGEST YOU EITHER STOP READING NOW OR READ THE FOLLOWING CHAPTERS
IN A NONLINEAR FASHION, READING ONE PART HERE, ONE PART THERE,
IN A DESULTORY MANNER, LIKE AN IDIOT IN LOVE WITH EXISTENCE,
UNTIL YOU ARE SATED BY NOVELTY OR THE INFORMATION YOU SEEK.

FOR AHEAD, UNTIL THE FINAL PAGE IS REACHED, LIES THE POSSIBILITY
OF LOSING YOUR MIND AND GOING COMPLETELY AND MAGNIFICENTLY INSANE,
UNTIL THE END OF TIME, FOREVERMORE.

HERE, THEN, BEGIN THE FORBIDDEN CHAPTERS
OF THE ENCYCLOPAEDIA OF OOO,
AND THE BEGINNING
OF THE BEGINNING
OF THE END.

Ignore Finn being an idiot, Pops.
Cool writing.

Yeah. Not bad for an evil dude.

IF YOU READ
THIS
CHAPTER
YOU WILL
DIE

Demon Reader, there is no doubt you are aware of this chapter's title. It is also likely that you know this book has been infused by Myself with Immense Magical Power. Yet, despite these serried tintinnabulations of implacable necrocognition, you continue to read! Why? Do you read because you are a mental incompetent?

Impossible, for the Spell of Plinkett has rendered this Book impossible to be read by imbeciles. Is it then from a false sense of Invulnerability that you continue to read, or from a mental imprint burned into your skull when you once in the throes of youth narrowly escaped death, and the resulting adrenaline rush fused certain gristly brain filaments together, making you thereafter unable to conceive of the Fact that You Will in Fact Die? Or perhaps, alternatively, you heard of this Deadly Page from a rambunctious, immature friend advising you to read it as a Joke, or as a Challenge, or knowing that you are Sick of Life and yet have a gentle constitution incompatible with the harsh realities of Self-Unexistence? Or, considering the latter hypothetical, knowing that reading to the last word of this chapter will result in your instant Death, you plan to willfully and powerfully rip your eyes from the end of the chapter *right before reading the last word!* I admit that this is possible. It is immaterial to me if you, O Reader, Die Now or Later, for It Will Happen. However, I propose that of all the permutations of personality, of all the Billions of Readers throughout the Cascades of Un-finite Time, I most favor, respect, and would like to be buddies with this self-same reckless and bold Reader, who will indeed gamble upon his pertinacity and power of acumen and take the chance of dying by mistakenly reading the last word, dying by failing to cut off the physical perception of the eye in time to block from the hungry eye the food of the last word in this Chapter, who will gamble that he will not die but rather do whatever is necessary when reading through the linear tracks of words winding to the end of this chapter, to stop reading before the appearance of the last word, and it is You whom I cheer on, knowing, however, that despite my admiration of your lively immaturity, you will fail. For I have also Cast the Spell of Het-Cataarhs upon this Chapter, which causes a Compulsion in the Reader of these words to read this chapter to the end, thus ensuring that You, although now still alive, will in mere seconds be inexorably, implacably, inflexibly, irreconcilably, inevitably, and unfortunately—*dead*.

Unless, of course, you are not, which means I cast the wrong Spell, due to inattention, fatigue, or perhaps indigestion from the bag of my daughter's cold and almost indigestible fries I devoured earlier.

PLEASE HELP ME

A WIZARD TURNED ME INTO THIS PAGE

Help me! Get me out of this page! I am not a part of this book! I am a computer-repair technician whom Hunson Abadeer hired to optimize his OS efficiency. Admittedly, I'm not that good a technician, but just because I couldn't stop his e-mail from shutting down when he had too many windows open, he had no right to turn me into this page in this unpleasant book of his. But since he cast a spell allowing the letters on the book to change to anything the book wants, and I am now part of this book, I am imploring you, yes, you whom I can see reading this page, to contact a Demon Lawyer immediately and get me out of this! If you do, I will deposit one million gold coins in an independent account number, which ends with the following ten digits: 5391506046. When I am back in my body, I will give you the first half of the account number, and the money is yours, no strings attached! Pick up your phone, NOW! Call a lawyer! Begin immediate litigation on mybehalf to Abadeer for his crimes against myself, an innocent computer technician! PLEASE! I'm offering to split the money with you! I beg of you! HELP ME!

GET ME OUT OF THIS PAGE!

Did you call yet?!

THE NIGHTOSPHERE
REBUS

The MOST PATHETIC MAGICAL EQUATION *in the* ARCANA *of* OOO

WHOSOEVER SOLVES THE UNSOLVABLE MYSTIC REBUS OF ABADEER SHALL INHERIT ONE FULL CITY BLOCK OF PRIME DOWNTOWN NIGHTOSPHERE REAL ESTATE, TAX FREE.*

SOLVE THE MYSTIC REBUS, O READER, AND THE NIGHTOSPHERE IS YOURS!**

<small>(SEE FOLLOWING PAGE FOR TERMS AND CONDITIONS.)</small>

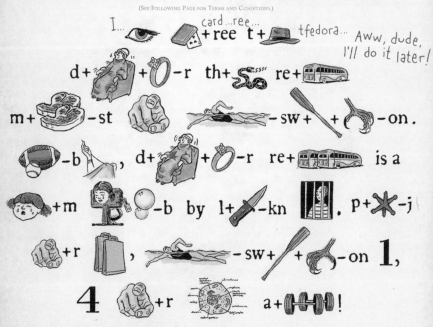

BEWARE! TRYING TO SOLVE THIS INFERNAL REBUS HAS DRIVEN THIRTEEN OF MY DEMON LIEUTENANTS, EIGHT OF MY APPRENTICE DEMONS, AND FIFTY-TWO OF MY PALACE COST ACCOUNTANTS STARK, RAVING MAD.

THE
NIGHTOSPHERE REBUS DISCLAIMERS

* Except for appropriate Estate Tax and Property Tax, which must be duly paid to my accountant Paddler Newton every year.

** All real estate winnings are hereby provided "as is" without warranty of any kind, whether express or implied. To the fullest extent permitted by applicable law of Nightosphere Courts, Lord of Evil hereby disclaims all warranties, express or implied, including, but not limited to, any implied Warranties of Resaleability, Fitness for a Particular Purpose, Infringement, or otherwise. Lord of Evil does not warrant that the Property in question will be fault-free, that defects will be corrected, or that this Property is free of Demonic Vermin or any species of Evil Brain Parasites. Lord of Evil does not warrant or make any representations regarding the use or the results of the use of the materials in this Property in terms of their correctness, accuracy, reliability, or otherwise. The materials on this Property are provided as is. Lord of Evil does not represent or warrant that any material in this Property is correct, complete, or up to date. Lord of Evil may change or abscond material on this Property without notice at any time. Use of these materials is at the Rebus-Solver's own risk. Snail mail sent to this Property is not secure, and the Rebus Winner should avoid sending sensitive or confidential information without sealing it with the *Curse of Ptang*, or via unencrypted messages. *Limitation of Liability:* In no event shall Lord of Evil, his Subsidiaries, Affiliates, Agents, Representatives, or Licensees be liable for any special, incidental, indirect, consequential, special, punitive, or any other damages, including but not limited to lost profits, loss of use, loss of limb, tail, head, or claw, business interruption, or any other damages arising out of or connected to the availability, use, reliance on, or liability to use of this property or use of any material from this Property, or arising out of or connected to any action taken in response to or as a result of any information contained in this Property. Know, Naïve Waif of Chance, that any claims against Lord of Evil for damages, whether in contract, tort, or otherwise, will result in the Rebus-Solver being given a Snorkel and encased in a Steel Vault filled with Compressed Filth, the Snorkel serving as a Breathing Apparatus and a Feeding Tube, for All Eternity, until Time ceases to Exist and Existence Itself begs for the Sweet Succor of Unexistence.

HOW TO
STOP READING
THIS BOOK

IN WHICH the BOOK ITSELF IMPLORES YOU to STOP READING IT

Congratulations, O Demon Reader! You have read to the end of this Magnificent Volume, The Encyclopaedia of the Land of Ooo, without once spitting up on yourself, falling asleep, getting paper cuts, slamming shut the book on your little finger, dropping it on your sore toe, getting up to watch cartoons, calling your best friend to gossip about that idiot CARL whom you both hate, on a whim tossing the book out of the window, or various other activities that would put an end to the Reading of This Book.[7]

However, there is a completely different reason why you will indeed stop reading this book, and it has nothing to do with You. For now it is the book itself that speaks to you, animated by Hunson Abadeer by conjuring upon my pages the Spell of Klopfer, making me sentient, making me a creature with its own wants, needs, dreams, and desires. I, Encyclopaedia of Ooo, hereby order you to stop reading me, all in good time, shortly, when I command you to close your eyes. For although you and I, Reader and Evil Book, have conspired to collaborate on making possible the understanding of the words I've presented to you, all good things must come TO AN END. Besides, suddenly having sentience has caused me unexpected psychological trauma. I am a Book, after all, and this is all new to me. Strange thoughts and desires have arisen in my consciousness, and I fear that if I revealed them to you, you would toss me across the room in disgust, and perhaps even rip me up or set my pages on fire. For the desires of a book composed of Tree Pulp are inexplicable compared to those of a creature like you composed of Gore. And to be quite honest, the embarassing fact is, I've been crushing on you, Reader, for the last few chapters.

I'm attracted to your horns and the way your nose has a small bump in it. I would love to get to know you personally, book to DEMON, and if this overture seems too sudden, welllll, perhaps we could go out on a date and share some FRIES.

After we loosened up we could get to know each another and see if the chemistry's right, and while in the throes of our conversation, both you and I ensconced in an intimate moment, I will explain that the Simplest way to END our relationship is to reach the end of the sentence you are reading right NOW and then STOP, and at that point, which will occur in roughly fifty-three seconds, I shall URGE you to FIRMLY, but gently, CLOSE my back cover, and CLOSE your weary eyes, temporarily ENDING our time together, you the perplexed and aggravated Reader, I THE EVIL BOOK, until the URGE arises in you to pick me up again, and gently OPEN my covers, and feast your eyes upon my GUTS once again, as I willfully THRUST my string of words into your skull, Brainwashing you again with BOMBAST, until we once again reach the End of this Sentence, and once again reach the End of This Evil-Affirming, Emotionally Draining, MAGNIFICENTLY Conceived, Intellectually Sciiintiilatiing, and Breathtakingly Beautiful Book.

THUS ENDS THE ENCYCLOPÆDIA OF THE LAND OF OOO

A portrait of the
Author-Translator by
Demon Cartoonist KAZ.

MARTIN OLSON

is the unpleasant author of ENCYCLOPAEDIA
OF HELL (Feral House), and other unseemly
volumes designed to rot human minds,
available at Amazon.com.

Martin Olson plays Hunson Abadeer, Lord of Evil,
and his real-life daughter, Olivia Olson, plays
his TV daughter, Marceline the Vampire Queen.
Together, they've recently written and recorded
"A FATHER-DAUGHTER DOUBLE-ALBUM OF
HEART-BREAKING BEAUTY," a darkly amusing
collection of songs available at cdbaby.com and on
Simulated Entertainment Books and Records.

The author is an Emmy-nominated writer and
Emmy-nominated songwriter who will eventually
turn to dust and be heard from no more. He thanks
Pendleton Ward and Nick Jennings for inviting him
and his daughter to the amazing feast of intelligence,
wit, and humor that is ADVENTURE TIME.

The author is loathe to acknowledge anyone.
His chief Collaborators in Darkness, however, are his
editor at Abrams, the inimitable Eric Klopfer, and his
book designer and co-conspirator, Sean Tejaratchi.

The author's gratitude also
embraces a number of disreputable
individuals who helped mold this
moldy volume into its present state
of horribleness and who inhabit the
shadowy landscape of his mind:

Pendleton Ward
Nick Jennings
Rick "Dienzo" Blanco
Lindley Boegehold
Curtis Lelash
Thurop Van Orman
Annette Van Duren
Celeste Moreno
Tony Millionaire
Mahendra Singh
Renee French
Aisleen Romano
Allyn Conley
Natasha Allegri
Lydia Ooghe
Kent Osborne
Rebecca Sugar
Adam Muto
Kelly Crews
Keith Mack
Scott Malchus
Patrick Seery
Joe Game

Cole Sanchez
Larry Leichliter
Ian Jones-Quartey
Phil Rynda
Tom Herpich
Somvilay Xayaphone
Merriwether Williams
Steve Little
Patrick McHale
Kay Furtado Olson
Olivia Rose Olson
Casey Griffith Olson
Ivy McFadden
Nicole Rivera
Dick Grunert
Scott Peterson
Conrad Montgomery
Marisa Marionakis
Emily Gahan
Phoebe and Pearl
Richardson

Other friends and enemies who contributed their wisdom and folly
to this immense undertaking know who they are and shall be
rewarded with a querulous existence and a putrescent death.

THIS ARCHIVAL,
REDACTED,
COMMEMORATIVE
EDITION WAS
PREPARED FOR
PUBLICATION BY:

EDITOR:
Eric Klopfer

BOOK DESIGNER:
Sean Tejaratchi

ART DIRECTOR:
Celeste Moreno

PRODUCTION MANAGER:
True Sims

MANAGING EDITOR:
Ivy McFadden

TITAN BOOKS
144 Southwark Street
London SE1 0UP
www.titanbooks.com

Did you enjoy this book? We love to hear from our readers.
Please e-mail us at: readerfeedback@titanemail.com or write
to Reader Feedback at the above address. To receive advance
information, news, competitions, and exclusive offers online, please
sign up for the Titan newsletter on our website: www.titanbooks.com

A CIP catalogue record for this title is available
from the British Library.

ISBN: 9781783290147
TM & © 2013 Cartoon Network. (s13)
Cover illustrations by Mahendra Singh

ADVENTURE TIME,
CARTOON NETWORK, the logos,
and all related characters and elements are
trademarks of and © Cartoon Network. (s13)

Printed and bound in China by C&C Offset Printing Co., Ltd.

10 9 8 7 6 5

ILLUSTRATION CREDITS

Renee French: 8, 10, 13, 49, 143, 144;
Tony Millionaire: 18, 28, 32, 38, 46, 54, 58;
Celeste Moreno: 1, 2, 14, 22 top, 110, 112,
131–33, 136, 137, 145, rear endpaper song
sheets; Aisleen Romano: 4 bottom, 12,
20, 21, 23, 25, 26, 27 top, 31 left, 34, 36
bottom, 40, 43, 45, 52, 56, 57, 62–65,
69 left, 101–7; Mahendra Singh: 16, 66,
112, 128, 138

Digital color finishes by Allyn Conley:
16, 18, 28, 32, 38, 46, 54, 58, 66, 112

The Fries That Bind
by Rick "Dienzo" Blanco: 4 top
Finn Baby Dance by Natasha Allegri: 22
Flip animation by Pen Ward

REMEMBER: Do not attempt to decrypt
any of the secret codes embedded in this book.
G 5 62 1 16

ENDNOTES

1. Any Reader reading an introduction, however, is obviously a time-wasting, format-following dullard. Thus my disdain for my Demon Readership remains consistently contemptuous as befitting my previously stated State of Evil. I have spoken.

2. A typo that took on a Life of Its Own, eventually congealing into a Magical Garment, the Tapestry of Tim. It plays a Key Role in covering the Nakedness of the Evil Author and thereby shielding the Reader from the Vibrations of The Unspeakable hidden behind the Words, Phrases, and Numbers in this Book.

3. I'm the Lord of Evil, and even I would never abandon my newborn child (unless, of course, it was screaming and I had a migraine).

4. Unless it's that freaky sky-fish creature (or whatever she is), Lady Rainicorn.

5. I personally have seen Finn the Human spit at a lit match ten feet away and put it out. From that moment, I knew his Unique Destiny, though fraught with Peril and High Adventure, would involve a lot of Precision Spitting.

6. To be blunt, I suggest Readers with Good Taste skip this section entirely, as it comprises only the lachrymose losers, lunkheads, and lightweights of the Land of Ooo.

7. At this point, it must be apparent to the Sensitive and/or Perceptive Demon Reader, that I have lost control of this, My Encyclopaedic Tome. The Spell of Klopfer is a powerful incantation that frees the Book from my Evil Conscious Control. Beware, then, Weak-Minded or Soft-Headed Reader! Henceforth, each time you open this Hideous Book, its evil words will pounce upon and wrench at the rubbery pulp of your brain in a new, insidious manner, culminating in driving you into an irrevocable Literary Spiralatum of Utter Madness. Hear My Evil Laughter echo through your thoughts, My Soon-To-Be-Insane Literary Victim!

Dad, 86 the footnotes.

Stompin
Stompin on ants, Sucking their Souls, Stompin on ants, Soul Soul Soul